Grandmother's Stories

How the Earth and Sky Began

Daniel Auger

ESCHIA
BOOKS

The Publisher: Eschia Books Inc.

Library and Archives Canada Cataloguing in Publication

Auger, Daniel, 1956–
Grandmother's stories: how earth and sky began / Daniel Auger.

ISBN 978-1-926696-17-1

1. Indians of North America—Canada—Folklore.
2. Legends—Canada. 3. Creation—Mythology. I. Title.

E98.R3A93 2011   398.2089'97   C2011-907092-8

Project Director: Kathy van Denderen
Cover Image: © Photos.com

Produced with the assistance of the Government
of Alberta, Alberta Multimedia Development Fund   **Government of Alberta** ■

We acknowledge the support of the Canada Council for the Arts
which last year invested $24.3 million in writing and publishing
throughout Canada.

Canada Council   Conseil des Arts
for the Arts   du Canada

PC: 5

To my grandmother, for imparting a sense of wonder in me as a child and for giving me the ability to look past what is in front of me and see the magic in life.

Contents

Part II: The Origins of the Natural World

Acknowledgements

To my publisher, without whom this book never would have been possible. Thank you for your encouragement.

And to all of my friends and family who helped me sort through my memories and vague recollections to fill in details I've forgotten and to take me back to the magic of my grandmother's stories.

Introduction

We all seek to understand the world around us. For the First Nations peoples of Canada, their understanding of the world was explained through stories. The story of creation, of how we came to exist in the universe, is one of the most common in human experience. In many of the stories in this book, you will most certainly recognize themes found in some of humanity's oldest traditions—the stories as old as time.

I was first introduced to these stories as a child. My grandmother, who was the greatest storyteller, passed these stories onto me. In her soft voice, she told stories of heroes and giants, of evil deeds and heroic tales. Sometimes the stories were short, sometimes long, but she always managed to keep me and my brother completely under her spell.

My grandmother seemed to have an endless supply of stories to tell. She visited us one time and told a story from one of the West Coast tribes; another time she told us a story by the Mi'kmac from the east or the Dene of the north. As a child, I never thought much of it, but as I grew up, I found out that my grandmother was a collector of stories. From an early age, she read anything she could get her hands on that related the tales of the tribes of North America, such as Franz Boas' translations of the West Coast tribal stories.

As my grandmother grew older, she collected stories from tribal elders across Canada and wrote them down in her own personal notebook. It was her hobby and her own special way of keeping the unique First Nations culture alive.

She wrote stories about the mischievous Raven, of the equally mischievous Coyote, of brave heroes, terrified men and mighty spirits. I often looked back to these stories while writing this book, recalling those nights when she told them to me. My grandmother is no longer of this world, but I like to think her voice remains in the words she passed down to me, which I now share with you. Her ragged notebook was an essential guidebook in compiling this book on the origin tales of Canada's First Nations.

For generations, these stories were a way to make sense of the world and provide an explanation for events that seemed incomprehensible. The most universal of those stories was how the earth and everything on it came into being. The modern mind looks to science and the Big Bang Theory as the explanation for how living things came into existence. While science can give the bare facts, I prefer stories in which gods and spirits create the world and all terrestrial life in creative and magical ways. In this book, you will find a variety of stories that explain and help us understand how certain aspects of the natural world were brought to life, from the grand creation of the universe to how the narwhal got its tusk.

As varied as many of these stories are, they often share the same themes and characters. While Native communities along the West Coast of Canada often have the mythical figure of Raven in their stories, and Plains tribes often refer to Coyote, the actual stories of creation themselves remain rather similar. But know that each story as a whole is unique to the culture of the region.

These stories gave First Nations people a foothold in the world—an explanation that made humans seem great and important in a great and eternal universe. They grounded our people to this world and the world to them. So I ask you to put aside your modern way of thinking and dive into these stories with an open mind and imagination.

Part I:
Tales of Creation

Out of Nothing Came Big Raven

OUT OF NOTHING CAME Big Raven and his wife. They were the first two living beings on earth, and their home was a small piece of land that floated through the darkness. For an unimaginable amount of time, Big Raven and his wife lived this way, with no other animals, no plants and no people to disturb their quiet world. There were no salmon, no bears, no trees, no wolves, no whales, no rising sun, no ivory moon—nothing but Big Raven and his wife.

Big Raven liked the silence and did not want to do anything to disturb his world. He and his wife lived this way for millennia until Big Raven's wife awoke one morning and said to her husband, "Existence has become dull and boring. We pass our time floating through the darkness on this little piece of dirt with nothing to amuse ourselves."

"What would you have me do about it?" asked Big Raven. "We create ourselves out of nothing, but I cannot create things in this world just to amuse you because you are bored."

His response did not make his wife happy.

"Lazy!" she screamed at her husband. "Get out there and create the rest of the world. This life is dull, and I can't live with only you anymore. Make the earth and the oceans and fill them with life. If you don't, I will leave you and you'll never hear from me again!"

"But, my dear wife, I cannot go out and create the earth so easily. It is beyond my power," replied Big Raven.

"You underestimate your abilities. You are Big Raven, but if you're too much of a coward to at least try to create the earth, then make me a companion to talk to and play with," ordered Big Raven's wife.

"Woman, you are too demanding! Our world is quiet, with nothing to disturb us. Why would you want to go and disrupt such a serene world?"

"Fine, then if you will not create something, I shall take up the matter myself," said Big Raven's wife.

To this, Raven simply laughed. "I will watch you closely and make sure that you do not interfere with the peaceful life we have."

For many days and nights, Raven watched over his wife during her waking hours and while she slept. Having neglected to rest himself, Big Raven's eyes grew heavy with sleep and for a brief moment his eyes closed. When he opened his eyes, he looked over to his wife and panicked when he saw that she no longer had the body of a raven.

He could hardly believe his eyes. Gone was her beautiful black coat of feathers. She was now covered in golden skin. Her sharp talons had shrivelled into a strange set of wiggling toes, her great black wings had shrunk, becoming two smooth arms, and her sharp beak had fallen off to reveal a sensuous pair of lips.

"My wife!" Raven cried. "What have you done?"

"Since you would not listen to me, I took matters into my own hands, and now I can create the companions to amuse us and to take care of us," his wife replied.

Jealous at his wife's sudden change in appearance, Big Raven tried desperately to alter his form. He tried his most powerful magic spells, he pulled at his feathers and he wiggled his talons, but nothing seemed to work. For days, Raven tried to change into the human form his wife had taken, but he had no success. He was so involved in trying to transform himself that he didn't notice his wife's belly had swollen to twice its normal size. While Raven was staring down at her belly, he saw two baby boys emerge from his wife.

Upon looking at Raven, the twin boys immediately began to cry and point at the strange-looking beast covered in feathers. "Mama, Mama!" they cried. "What's that?"

"Why, children, that is your father," replied the boys' mother.

The twins looked at each other, then at their mother, and then their eyes fell on Raven and they burst out laughing. "Ha! Our father? How could this feathered, black-eyed beast possibly be our father?" said one of the twins as they poked and pulled at Raven's feathers and beak.

"Boys, leave your father alone. Have some respect and stop laughing!" screamed their mother.

Unable to take any more of the laughing, Big Raven left his lodge and took to the peace of the skies. Flying overhead, he called down to his wife. "So you have created humans. But as you can see, they will need to be taught how to live and behave," said Raven. "These people will grow and multiply—you have forced me to go out and create a world for them to inhabit and populate. I will go now. I might not return, but I shall take one of my sons with me on the journey and show him what is to be done in the name of his people and maybe they will learn to respect their father."

Raven swooped down out of the air, placed one of his sons on his back and flew off into the distance. At first, the boy was scared of his father who looked nothing like him, but he soon began to trust him.

Big Raven told his son of the ways of the world. He did so for many years, and by the time Big Raven had taught his son everything he knew, the young boy had become a man.

"My son, once you were a tiny child who laughed out of ignorance and cowered in fear because you lacked courage. But since you have clung to my back, I have taught you everything I know, and now you are ready to go forth into the world," said Raven. "I created myself, and now I shall create a world for you to live in. First, I shall create the waters."

"How will you make the waters?" asked his son.

Raven was thinking about his son's question, and in that quiet moment, his thoughts turned to his wife. He had not seen her in many years. His eyes filled with tears, and he cried so much that his tears began to pour down onto the world. When he stopped crying, he found he had created the oceans.

"Father, this is wonderful!" said his son. "But I will need some land to put my feet upon and to build a home."

Raven thought about his son's words. He then strained really hard and defecated. His feces flew down out of the sky and landed in the water, forming a huge island. He continued to circle the earth, and everywhere his feces fell, new land sprang up out of the waters.

His son gazed out over the lands and marvelled at his father's creations. Where there was nothing before, he now saw miles of coastline, massive mountains that reached for the heavens and long stretches of flat land that melted into the horizon. Big Raven descended out of the sky and placed his talons on the newly formed earth.

"Father, what you've done is incredible, and although I know you are tired, I have another request," said Raven's son.

"What is it? Surely I cannot have missed anything. I have given you land and water. What more do humans need?"

"The lands are barren," said his son, pointing to the horizon. "I have nothing to build a home and no animals to hunt for food. Are you not hungry, Father?"

Raven looked at his son and knew that his thin layer of skin could not protect him against the elements and that he himself had not eaten anything since he had created this new world.

Big Raven flew into the sky again with his son on his back, and together they looked over his creation. Raven said to his son, "Take some of my feathers and throw them down to earth. They will become the trees that will grow to form great forests."

His son pulled out a few feathers from his father's back and threw them down to earth. The feathers flew down like arrows and stuck deep into the ground. The feathers immediately turned into trees and multiplied, blooming a sea of green across the landscape. However, Raven had only so many feathers to offer, and as a result, many parts of earth were left without forests.

Big Raven and his son descended from the skies and gazed upon the land Raven had created.

"I have done well," said Raven. "Now I will create the animals that will populate earth and provide you with food."

Big Raven grabbed a few trees, took up his axe and began to chop at them. With a few strokes, he reduced the trees to a pile of wood chips. He took some of the chips in his hands and threw them into the oceans. They were carried off by the currents to all the parts of the world and were transformed into whales, walruses, seals and all the creatures of the seas.

Big Raven took another handful of wood chips and threw them up into the air. Carried off into the wind, the chips floated high into the sky where they transformed into eagles, gulls, hawks and other creatures of the sky. Raven gathered more chips and spread them across the lands, and they, too, transformed, becoming deer, bears, squirrels and every other kind of animal that walks on land.

"There, my son. Now you have food for your belly and animal skins to clothe yourself," said Big Raven. "I have provided everything you need to survive out in the world."

Raven watched as his son fashioned a lodge, hunted the animals, procured plenty of food and made clothing to keep himself warm. Big Raven, however, noticed that there was one problem.

"I have given you everything you need, but I have failed to provide you with a companion," Big Raven said to his son. "But I don't know how I can do this."

Big Raven flew up into the air and perched himself on a branch of a nearby tree and quietly wondered how he could provide a companion for his son. He could see that his son's spirit was lonely and that he needed a purpose. Through many sunrises and sunsets, Raven pondered this question, but he could not come up with an answer. He had almost given up when one day a small Spider Woman crawled up to him.

"I believe I can help you with your problem," she said. "I am Spider Woman, and I have been listening to you as you pondered out loud on how you might provide a companion for your son. Look at him down there. He wanders about with no purpose. Lonely and frustrated. I can make him whole."

"How can you help?" laughed Big Raven. "You are just a tiny creature. Gaze upon me. I am the creator of all things, and I have created myself out of nothing. How could a little thing like you possibly create something of value?"

"Your ego is bigger than your brain, oh great Big Raven," mocked Spider Woman. "Do not be so quick to judge."

"Then prove to me what you can do," demanded Raven.

"I have watched your son, and what he needs is a woman. So I will give birth to daughters and give one of them to your son."

"But you are too small to give birth to a human," replied Raven.

"Again, you judge too quickly," said Spider Woman.

Big Raven could hardly believe his black eyes as Spider Woman grew 10 times her size. He watched as something inside her belly writhed and squirmed beneath the skin's surface. With one loud cry, Spider Woman gave birth to two baby girls. They grew into two beautiful women right before his eyes. Raven peered at their bodies, taking in every aspect of their beautiful hair, full lips, ample breasts and delicious curves. It was at this time that Raven's son approached him.

"Father, what sort of creatures are these? They look like me in certain ways, yet they are most definitely not like me," said Raven's son with his eyes firmly focused on the two young women.

"Choose one woman for your companion. You no longer shall roam this earth alone," said Raven.

"Be warned, son of Raven," exclaimed Spider Woman. "My daughter must be looked after. You must give her shelter, clothing and plenty of food."

"You have my word," said Raven's son. "You have taken me out of loneliness and given me purpose. I swear on my life that I will protect her."

Raven's son left his father's side and returned home with the woman he had chosen. A few days later, curious at how his son was doing with his new companion, Raven took to the skies and flew to his son's home. Big Raven arrived in the early morning light and peered into the lodge to find that his son had slept the night curled up on the opposite side from the woman.

"Must I teach the boy everything...?" thought Raven.

Raven quietly crept to his son's bed and whispered into his ear, "Go outside and watch what is to be done."

The beautiful woman lay naked on the ground and drew Raven's body close to hers when he approached. Caressing her body, Raven gently opened her legs and had his way with her. He did this over and over, from sunrise to sunset. Outside, his son watched, growing jealous with each passing moment. He entered the lodge and said to his father, "It is time for you to leave."

"Yes, it is," replied Raven. "Take your place beside this beautiful creature."

Raven's son took his place beside his companion. "I don't know what to do," he said to her.

"Don't worry. I will show you," replied the woman.

Raven left his son to his education in the new world he had created and took Spider Woman's other daughter to his home so that his other son could have a companion of his own. After spending such a long time away from his own wife, Big Raven also needed some companionship.

Thus Big Raven made himself out of nothing and then created the oceans, the lands, the trees, the plants and the animals for the first people, all of whom are his children. Big Raven returned to his wife and continues to this day to watch over his chosen people.

The Arrival

LONG AGO, ONLY THE ANIMAL people lived on earth. They were neither fully animal nor fully people but a mix of both. Life was peaceful, and there were no wars. Then the Creator, Glooscap, called all the leaders of the animal tribes to a grand council. The great Glooscap told them that he was happy with their work on earth but that it was time for the world to change.

He said, "There will be a new kind of people in this world soon, and they will spread far and wide across the lands. We must prepare for their arrival."

"What do you mean 'prepare'?" someone asked.

"I know some of you, like Crane and Bear, already have names, but some of you don't.

When the people arrive, they will need to know your names, so at first light tomorrow you will all return to my lodge and choose new names. The order is first come, first serve," decreed Glooscap to the animal people.

After listening to what Glooscap had told them, all the animals began discussing what names they would like to take. Each animal wanted to have the most powerful and respected of names and vowed to be the first in line. Crane was the most vocal of all the animals, boasting that he would be first in line to take the most respected name. He wanted a new name after living with the name "Crane" for so many years. "Crane" had become synonymous with trickery, deception and foolishness. He was the great imitator and no one, not even the rat, wanted to take his name.

"I'll be the first in line to choose a new name, then someone else will know the shame and stigma of my name," said Crane. "I'll choose the name of Bear and become the most powerful animal to walk on land. Or should I choose the name Eagle and rule the skies?"

"But, brother," said Crow. "No one wants your name, and everyone will fight to be first in line, just like you. You are skinny and weak. How will you push your way past the stronger?"

"Don't you worry about that," replied Crane. "I might not be strong, but sometimes the deception associated with my name can come in handy."

"Just be warned," said Crow. "Whatever name you want to choose is not yet yours. You better get some rest and be awake at first light, or you will remain forever with your burden, and when the people come, they will mock you."

This was wise advice from Crow, but Crane did not pay any attention to his words. He was much too involved in his own schemes. While the rest of the animal people went off to bed, Crane had other plans. "I will stay up all night so as not to be the last of the animals to choose a name. I will be the greatest animal in all the world," he thought.

Crane returned to his lodge and continued to dream of all the things he would do once he had chosen his new name. "Tomorrow I will become someone respected, someone whose name will forever be remembered in the annals of our history. When the first peoples arrive, they will fear and respect me. I'll do great things with my new name. I think I'll become Bear and devour my enemies in one bite," he said out loud to himself. "No, maybe I'll become Eagle, so I can soar above the clouds. This will be a difficult choice to make, but luckily I'll have all night to think it over while the others sleep comfortably in their beds."

Crane went outside and gathered a load of fire-wood for the long night ahead and sat down to warm himself beside the fire he had made. He pondered what name he would choose in front of Glooscap in the morning. Crane started the evening wide eyed and full of excitement, but as the night wore on, the fire began to hypnotize him. His eyes grew heavy, and slowly they shut. After a while, he opened his eyes and noticed that it was no longer dark. He had slept all night.

In a panic, Crane rushed to the lodge of the Creator, burst through the door and found no other animal waiting. "Could it be that I am the first in line?" he thought. Walking up to where the Creator was sitting, Crane pronounced, "Since I'm the first one here, I'd like to take the name of the mighty Bear."

"The name you have selected was chosen already," said Glooscap.

"Then I shall take the name of the majestic Eagle and fly free in the skies," proclaimed Crane.

"The owner of that name flew off into the sun this morning."

"Then I will take the name of the noble Wolf," said Crane anxiously.

"You're too late for that name as well. Wolf silently disappeared into the forest with his family," said Glooscap.

Crane's pride-filled heart suddenly sank with despair. "How about Owl, Beaver or Moose?"

The Creator just shook his head. All the names had already been taken, even Mosquito and Rat—only the name "Crane" was left.

"Do not despair, noble Crane, for it was my will that you missed all the great names. I have saved a special distinction for you. You are to become the protector of the first people," said Glooscap. "Spread across the lands are a great many beasts and monsters that will terrorize and kill the people so that they do not prosper. It is to you that I give the magical powers to defeat the beasts and teach the people how to survive in the world. With this power you can change into anything and do all sorts of magical things. You are only limited by your mind. You might have missed out on a powerful name, but there is great honour in the task you have been assigned."

Crane left the lodge of Glooscap feeling much better. He had become an important chief after all! When Glooscap created the first tribe, Crane walked among them and boasted of his new role on earth. He told them how important he was, and if they needed anything from him, they were to just ask and he would appear.

But nothing had changed for Crane. He was still the same prideful creature, often looking out for his own interests. He did fulfill his duties to Glooscap and teach the first peoples the ways of the world and protect them from the evil beasts, but every now and again he fell back into his old ways. However, in Crane's mind, he was the chief of all peoples, the most powerful among them, designated by the Creator to look after them.

Earth Held by Four Corners

THE GREAT ISLAND THAT IS the earth once floated alone deep within a giant ocean. It was suspended by four magical cords that hung down from the sky, and even though it was made of solid rock, it was lighter than air. The Creator had pulled up the earth from the bottom of the ocean and attached the magical cords. But like all living things in nature—except for the great Creator—each must have an ending.

When the earth grows old and worn out, the people will all die and the cords will break, letting the earth sink back down into the depths of the ocean. All will again be water and sky.

Long ago when no spirit walked the earth, all the animals lived above in the sky kingdom, but it was a crowded place and many of them wanted to have more room. They could see that the island called earth was vast and empty, but they did not know if it was made to give life. As there was no light on earth, a hole in the floor of the sky kingdom had to be opened to let down some light. When this faint light was cast over the dark landscape, the animals felt it was safe enough to send down several of the birds to fly over the land and report back on what they saw.

Blue Jay was the first to venture into the land below the sky. He found most of the land to be soft and wet. "If the buffalo were to descend to earth, they would surely get stuck in the mud," Blue Jay thought to himself. Finding no place to perch, he flew back up to the sky world.

The animals up in the sky waited several years for the earth to dry out. At long last, they decided to send Eagle down to earth to see if the land had dried out. Eagle flew all over the land looking for a proper spot on which to perch, but the ground was still too wet. He flew closer to the ground to get a closer look at the soil, and as he did, his mighty wings hit the ground and sent the soft soil up into the sky, creating the mountains and the valleys.

When the animals from up above saw what Eagle was doing, they called out for him to return to the sky world lest he make mountains all over the earth.

This is why certain parts of the earth remain full of mountains today.

After the animals waited another few years, the earth finally became dry and was ready for them to inhabit. They descended from the sky and arrived on earth, but there was no light. The animals sent White Raven up to the sky to find a source of light. White Raven, at the time, had the most brilliant coat of white feathers and was widely considered the most beautiful of all birds.

White Raven flew up into the sky and yelled out, "Oh, great Creator. Your subjects are in need of light down on earth. Could you help your poor creatures in our time of need?"

The answer came out of thin air. "You must seek out the old hag of the sky kingdom," commanded the Creator. "She is the keeper of the light and will not part with it willingly. Go to her, but how you get the light is your problem. I shall not meddle in earthly affairs. Take a path to the east and you will find her."

White Raven began his journey to the home of the old hag. For days, he walked through the empty expanse of the sky kingdom and thought it was a beautiful place now that all the animals had departed. There was a lot of space for him to roam, it was quiet, and most important of all, there was no one to tell White Raven what to do, since he liked to live by his own rules. Putting aside those thoughts, White Raven continued down a path to the east until he came to an ugly, rundown lodge, which he thought had to be the home of the old hag. White Raven circled the lodge several times before finally deciding on a direct approach.

"Is anyone home?" he called, but no answer came.

"Is there anyone home? I have travelled far!" bellowed White Raven again. When he still did not get a response, White Raven transformed himself into the form of a weary but handsome traveller and repeated his request.

A few minutes passed before the door opened a crack and a raspy voice whispered, "Go away. No visitors."

White Raven then tried to use his talent for words in order to enter her home. "My dear beautiful lady," he said confidently, "you're obviously a woman of great wisdom. I have only come to ask for a little food and water as I have been travelling for a long time. May I come into your home and rest my weary feet? I will tell you great stories of adventure and danger in exchange for a little kindness."

The old woman looked over the traveller several times before she pushed open the door and let him inside.

"Why do you travel in these parts?" hissed the old hag. "No one has come by my lodge for a long time, and all the animals seemed to have departed suddenly."

"This is why I am travelling, my dear," replied the traveller as he took a seat by the fire. "One day the sky kingdom was filled with life and plenty of animals to hunt, but now I can't even find a simple little mouse."

While White Raven recounted stories to the old hag of his travels, he scanned the room for the source of light the Creator said was in her possession.

"Might you have any food to eat?" asked the traveller. As he looked about the room, he spotted a box sitting in the corner underneath a pile of furs, but it was no ordinary box. It was carved in the most artistic of manners and the lid was painted a bright red. White Raven knew the box had to be the place where she hid the light.

"No, I have been without food for a few days," relied the old hag.

"Well, I wasn't going to tell anyone, but not too far from here I saw a deer down by a lake. I made sure not to scare it, but if you hurry, the deer will most likely still be there," said the traveller. "Take my spear and go kill the deer so that we might eat. I would go, but my feet are covered in sores and I cannot hunt. I will stay here and tend to the fire."

The old hag agreed, but before she left, she told the stranger that if he touched anything of hers, there would be trouble. White Raven of course did not listen to her warning. The moment she closed the door behind her, he went straight for the box in the corner of the room.

"It seems rather light," he thought as he lifted it out from underneath the pile of furs.

Examining the box carefully, White Raven gently lifted the lid. He saw a tiny bag tied at the top with a piece of string. After removing the bag, he put the box down on the floor. With the small bag in his hands, he untied the string. He had barely opened up the bag when a brilliant light shot out and illuminated the cabin. White Raven quickly resealed the bag and was about to leave with his prize when the old hag burst through the door.

"Thief!" she cried. "I knew I was mistaken to trust you. I will use my magic to turn you into the most hideous of beasts."

White Raven was trapped. The old hag was blocking the door and there were no windows to escape from. He frantically scanned the room and saw that his only way out was through the chimney. White Raven transformed back into his original form and quickly flew up through the soot-filled smoke stack and out into the open air. He had escaped with the light, but in the process, his once brilliant white coat of feathers turned as black as night. From that day, he was known only as Raven.

Raven made his way back down to earth and presented the other animals with his discovery. Eagle flew into the sky and constructed a pathway that the light could travel on every day from east to west. Bear, the strongest of all the animals, took the sack containing the light, removed the golden orb that they called the sun and tossed it up into the sky where it landed on the pathway, where it remains to this day. The sun follows this path every day and returns on the other side in its starting place. It will do so until the world and everything in it falls back into the ocean when the four cords are cut.

With animals now plentiful on earth, the Creator created trees, grasses, fruit and grains for all the animals to eat. For many years, the animals lived in peace with one another. Then one winter, a terrible storm blew through the land and the animals began to starve for lack of food. They searched and searched but could only find enough food to ease the pains of hunger. Fox, one of the swiftest and most cunning of all the animals, was sent out to look for food.

Fox searched the frozen waste lands for several days but found nothing to eat. Then one day, he came across a buffalo that had recently died from hunger. Fox had never before thought of eating the flesh of another animal, but his hunger pains were too powerful to resist. Fox greedily fed on the remains of the buffalo, and from that day forth some animals chose to eat the flesh of others, and some preferred to eat the leaves and roots of plants.

This is how the earth, the animals and light came to be formed in the time before people. The earth remains held by the four corners, but one day the cords will break and all will be returned to the dark waters below.

Raven Separates Creation

LONG AGO BEFORE THE TIME of our people, there existed no divisions in the world. The worlds of the animals and the spirits were one. All the creatures of the earth, sky and water were connected, and all beings could pass freely between them. Life was always this way and had been since time began.

In this world long ago, an old hermit lived in a house on the banks of a river with his only child, a daughter. They could often be heard fishing, and when the daughter walked down to the river to wash clothes, she would sing the most beautiful songs. This was all that was known of the old man and his daughter. No one knew what he looked like or whether his daughter was as ugly as a frog or as beautiful as the sunrise because the world was trapped in darkness. No light fell onto any corner of the earth. It was as if those who inhabited the earth walked about with their eyes closed or were blind-folded. Light had once been present in the universe but long ago it disappeared, and ever since, the inhabitants of the earth simply stumbled about in the black void.

The person responsible for the disappearance of the light was the old man who lived down by the river with his daughter. In his house, he had a small box in which he had managed to trap all the light in the universe. As a young man, he used to love to play out in the sunlight and proudly display his youthful physique, but as he grew older and his beauty began to fade, he resented the light of a new day because he could not stop the passage of time. He decided to steal all sources of light so that no know would be able to see how ugly he had become.

Raven, who had always existed and will exist for-ever, was not happy living in the dark. He remem-bered the times before the light had gone from the universe, when he had gathered up tasty morsels of fish and other pleasures of the day. Raven now spent his life stumbling about in the blackness of space, eating only what he happened to trip over. He did not enjoy any of the passions that life offered. He was, after all, the great trickster and took great pleasure in playing in the affairs of others, but it's difficult to be cunning when you are blind. Having to live his life in the dark carried on for years, until one day Raven's bumbling took him close to the home of the old man and his daughter.

Walking along the banks of the river, Raven's ears caught the faint sound of a voice whispering in the wind. Someone was singing. Although he couldn't see, he recognized the voice as that of a woman, and Raven had to investigate further to find out if she was as beautiful as her voice.

As Raven drew closer to the sound of the woman's voice, the song abruptly ended, and he could hear footsteps moving away from him and then a door closing. Feeling his way through the dark, Raven came upon the wall of the house. He could make out what the people inside were saying. "Father, I was down by the river washing our clothes and I think I heard someone," said a woman's voice.

"Fear not, daughter, for I have stolen the light from the world so they will never find us. It is mine forever, and I'll never let it slip from my grasp. Because of me, the world shall not judge you by your looks. Whether beautiful or homely, you nor I will never know..." said the old man.

Shocked at the revelation that the old man had stolen the light, Raven decided instantly, even before the old man had finished his sentence, that he was going to steal the light back. The only problem for Raven was how he was going to get it. He didn't know how he would get into the house to steal the light.

Every time the father or daughter came out of the house, the door closed shut and Raven was never able to find the door. He figured it must have been cursed by dark magic. Driven by the desire to steal the light and to lay his eyes on the old man's daughter, Raven knew he had to come up with a different way to enter the house. This was not a problem for Raven because he was the most cunning creature in the universe.

Alongside the river not far from the house, Raven waited until he heard the gentle footsteps of the old man's daughter as she walked to the river to get their daily supply of water. It was at this time that Raven transformed himself into a tiny fish and managed to get swept up into the container the girl had dipped into the water. Thirsty from carrying the water back to her house, the girl took a drink from the container, and in the process Raven slid down her throat.

Wiggling his way through her insides, Raven found a soft comfortable spot in her belly, where he then transformed himself into a small human being. Exhausted by the transformation, Raven went to sleep for several months, and while he slept, he slowly grew in size.

The girl was confused about the changes happening to her body and kept her condition a secret from her father lest he become angry with her. But the day came when she could keep the secret no longer. After about nine months of sleep, Raven finally awoke and emerged from the loins of the girl with a noisy cry.

At first, the old man was furious when the child was born because Raven cried and screamed all day long. But strangely enough, the old man and his daughter loved him and treated him with tenderness. Although Raven felt warmly toward his new family, he never forgot his original plan. As he grew and began to walk about the house on his own, Raven felt his way through the darkness hoping to find where the old man had hidden the light. Then finally one day, Raven found what he was looking for.

In the corner of the house sat a large wooden box, and when Raven had his chance, he opened it up, but all he found inside was another box. The old man heard his chest being opened and immediately scolded the young boy. Raven began to cry and begged his grandfather to show him what was inside the second box, but the old man would not allow anyone to see his precious treasure.

However, Raven was never one to give up, and for several days he begged and pleaded with the old man to reveal the contents of the box. In time, the old man's heart began to melt at Raven's passionate pleas, and he agreed to open the box.

Raven's heart pounded with excitement when he heard the old man open the second box, then a third, then a fourth until finally, after what seemed an infinite number of boxes, the old man lifted a beautiful golden ball of light into the air. Light flooded the house in an instant, giving the old man only a glimpse of his grandson before the boy suddenly transformed before his eyes. The hands that once hugged his grandfather turned into mighty wings, the mouth that pleaded and cried grew into a huge beak, and the soft skin that his mother loved to touch turned into a coat of black feathers.

Raven flew into the air, and in one quick swoop he snapped up the light with his talons. He turned his head to get a look at the old man's daughter, who turned out to be a beautiful woman. He then flew up the chimney out into the open. Where there was once darkness, Raven had brought light. As he flew higher, the world beneath him revealed itself. Rivers sparkled as they rushed along the landscape, flowers bloomed and turned to great the light, and mountains cast dark shadows across the land.

Raven was so enthralled with the beauty of the world that he forgot about the light he held within his talons. The light slipped from his grasp and fell to the rocky ground below. He tried to catch the light, but it was too late. The ball of light smashed against a rock and broke into pieces. Upon breaking, the pieces of light immediately bounced up into the sky, where two large pieces lodged into the sky to become the sun and the moon, and a million little pieces of light became the stars.

Raven shrugged his shoulders at the loss of his prize and flew off in search of something to eat and possibly someone to trick.

The Great Flood

WITH LIGHT RETURNED TO the world, Raven focused his attentions on pleasing his appetites. He flew to a thin strip of dry land along the coast and gorged himself for days on the juicy treats that constantly washed up on the shore.

Raven had earned his meal after stealing the light from the old man. The light had brought the world back into existence. The sun blanketed the land in warmth during the day, and at night the moon and the stars sparkled in the darkness. The proper rhythms of the earth were in balance, and Raven was happy to reap the tasty rewards it offered.

All was well in the world for some time, but then Raven noticed that the rains began to fall less often, and when rain fell, there was less of it. Without the rains, the river and lakes soon began to evaporate under the sun, and the ocean receded from the shores. The fish in the waters began to die, the trees became brittle and fell to the ground, and Raven became thirsty.

He flew high into the sky to look for any source of water he could find. He soared high up into the mountains and saw that the snows had disappeared from their peaks. He flew above the deep valleys and could see nothing but mud and rocks where once flowed mighty rivers. Raven flew on, hoping that he could find lakes that were still full of water, but again the landscape was bare.

Everywhere Raven travelled, he found nothing but drought and despair. The fields of flowers were wilted and dried. The forests were no longer healthy and green but yellow and bare. Raven would have cried at the sight but could not make any tears because he himself was also beginning to dry up.

After weeks of searching for water, Raven became tired. Sitting on the banks of what used to be his favourite river, he heard a deep grumbling noise off in the distance. At first he paid no attention to it, but then he heard it repeatedly and ever so faintly. "Grrbbbb, Grrrbbbt," went the sound. Naturally curious, Raven decided to investigate further.

Using what little energy he had left, Raven took to the skies and used his sensitive ears to guide him toward the mysterious noise. For hours he beat his tired wings, and just as he was about to fall from the sky, his keen eyes spotted what was surely the last green valley on earth. Raven landed in a beautiful meadow that was alive with the sounds of nature. Flowing water, chirping birds and the coolest of breezes floated down from the mountain. Raven wondered why he had not found this place before, and then the deep grumbling sound caught his attention once again.

"Grrrbbb, Grrrbbbt."

Raven looked all around him for the source of the noise and found an enormous frog whose stomach was almost bursting to capacity sitting at the top of a hill. As the frog lay asleep on the wet earth, Raven noticed he would move every so often, and Raven could hear water sloshing about in his belly. The frog opened his mouth and belched out, "Grrrbbb, Grrrbbbt," followed by a gush of water.

Raven quickly moved closer and took a sip of the water on the ground. It was the best water he had ever drank. In his excitement, Raven forgot to keep quiet and woke the giant frog.

With a grumble and a moan, the frog opened his eyes and looked down at Raven lapping away at the water on the ground. The frog opened his mouth and spoke.

"Who dares drink my water?" yelled the frog, spitting water as he spoke. "You have no right to take what is mine."

"You're taking more than you need," replied Raven. "The world is dying without water, and here you sit, fat and unwilling to give even a drop."

This angered the frog, and he lashed out at Raven with his long tongue. Raven avoided the strike and laughed at the fat frog. "Caw! Caw! You're too slow."

"The water is mine," said the frog, after sticking out his tongue to collect the water that flew from his mouth.

"Water cannot be owned by just one person. It is free like the air we breathe and the sunshine on our faces," said Raven.

But the frog wouldn't listen. All he kept saying was, "Mine, Mine, Mine!"

"Your greed has overtaken your senses. If you won't listen to reason, I shall have to force you to return all the water to the world," said Raven.

"Who are you to threaten me, Raven? I have the power, so I will do what I want," said the frog, laughing. "Now leave while I continue collecting what is mine."

It was then that Raven knew what he had to do. As the frog continued to lap at the waters surrounding him, Raven began to throw branches, rocks and dirt into the beast every time it opened his mouth.

The frog's thirst for water was so ravenous that he did not notice what Raven was throwing into his mouth. When Raven had thrown enough things into the frog's mouth, he simply sat back and waited.

The effect took only a minute. The frog's eyes widened, his face contorted, and his slimy hands began rubbing his belly.

"I don't feel so well," said the frog.

"It seems you have taken too much into your belly. You not only swallowed water but twigs and rocks too," replied Raven.

"I...am...in pain!" moaned the liquid-filled beast. "You must help me."

Raven knew he had the frog right where he wanted him. "Why should I help you?" he asked. "You strike at me with your tongue and deny me a refreshing drink. I should let you suffer for all eternity."

"Please make this pain stop," said the frog, writhing on the ground.

"No!" replied Raven. "Not unless you give up your water."

"Never!" cried the frog in obvious pain. "It's mine."

"Then suffer," said Raven.

The frog moaned and wailed for several hours, hoping the pain would go away, but his discomfort grew worse. The frog pleaded with Raven for his help.

"You're only pretending to be in pain so that I might help you," said Raven.

"No, I promise. I've learned my lesson. Now please help stop my pain," pleaded the frog.

Raven agreed. He got closer to the great beast and started poking at the frog's soft belly with his beak. When nothing happened on the first strike, Raven poked harder, and this time a huge stream of water squirted out of the frog's mouth. The water landed on the ground and flowed out of the valley to become a mighty river.

"Hold still, Frog, or I won't be able to free you from your pain," said Raven.

"You are doing this on purpose!" screamed the frog.

"I am not. Now quit moving," ordered Raven, again jabbing his beak into the belly of the frog. Another gush of water spewed out of the frog's mouth, shooting over the mountains where it froze and became ice and snow.

Raven pushed even harder once more, and a torrent of water issued out of the large beast's mouth. It covered the valleys, forming thousands of lakes. Everywhere the water travelled, the earth soaked it up, and the flowers, trees and grasses instantly sprung back to life.

"Good news, Frog! I think I have found the source of your pain," said Raven.

"Oh, thank the heavens! Please remove whatever it is."

Raven used his powerful beak to tear open the frog's belly. A torrent of water spewed out of the frog and spread across all the land. It flooded the valleys, filled the oceans and washed across the prairies. The land lay submerged for days until the earth drank its fill.

"How do you feel now?" Raven asked the frog.

"Oh, thank you, powerful Raven. I feel so much better. I can move around and jump once again," said the frog. "I never again want to experience such pain."

"Good. Remember this, and never again steal all the water in the world," warned Raven.

Raven, however, was not trustworthy and he didn't tell the frog that he had left a rock in his belly so that if he ever drank all the water again, his pain would return.

Raven left the frog in the valley and flew up high into the air. He could see that the forests bloomed with life and colour, and the rivers overflowed. The otters, the salmon, the bears and all the other creatures of the earth looked to the sky as Raven flew overhead. They thanked him from what he had done.

Raven flew back to his home on the coast, where he rested and gorged himself on the bounty that washed up on shore. He sat on his perch and gazed out proudly upon the world he had helped to create. Life on earth was in full bloom and he had plenty to eat, but something was missing.

As beautiful as the world now looked, bathed in light and teeming with life, Raven found it all quite boring. One day, under a clouded sky, Raven waddled down to the beach, his dark eyes darting randomly over the shores looking for anything to amuse himself, but all he found was more of the same.

The boredom was difficult for Raven to handle as he was a curious being and loved to involve himself in the affairs of others. With a sigh, he folded his wings behind his back, put his head down and walked back to his home to sleep the boredom away.

Raven and the Clam

RAVEN AWOKE ONE DAY, looked out at the beautiful emptiness and let out a heavy sigh. He was bored. After eating breakfast, he decided to take to the sky to kill some time. He flew inland, over the mountains and down into the valley where he had pierced the belly of the frog.

When the guilty frog saw Raven flying above him, he croaked out, "Soorrrry, soorrrry."

Raven continued toward the coast but could find nothing to relieve him from his boredom. The bears and the deer all busied themselves with their lives, and the otters and beavers quietly passed their days lounging in the calm waters. Raven tried to talk to the seal and the walrus, but they just laughed at him and shook their heads.

He even tried talking to the spirit of the sun and the moon, but they ignored him.

Raven was flying home along the coastline when he heard a noise he had never heard before. The muffled cries sounded like a baby seal, but it wasn't a seal. Raven peered out at the expanse of beach that lay beneath him. Everything appeared as it should. He was about to give up looking for something to amuse himself with when a ray of light reflected off something on the beach and hit him directly in the eyes. Raven had never before seen anything so bright on the beach. He could not pass up the curiosity.

Diving out of the air, Raven landed on the beach next to the strange object. Inspecting the alien flotsam that stuck partly out of the sand, Raven recognized it as a clamshell, though it was larger. Only a small portion of the shell stuck out of the sand, but he could tell that it was 10 times the normal size of any shell and was a brilliant white.

"It must have been revealed by the floodwaters," thought Raven. "I must know more." While Raven was digging out the giant shell, he heard the muffled cry again. It was coming from the shell, and the more he dug, the louder the cries became. After about an hour of digging, Raven unearthed a huge white-and-silver-speckled clamshell.

Raven strutted around the shell like a mountain lion around a freshly killed deer, proud at his discovery. He pecked at the mouth of the clam with his sharp beak, but the giant shell obviously did not want to reveal its secrets inside. Raven walked around the shell, poking and prodding for what seemed like hours. With each passing minute, whatever lay inside became increasingly agitated, rocking the shell back and forth on the beach.

Force was not going to work against such a large and powerful creature—using force wasn't any fun anyway, and Raven preferred to use other methods.

Placing his beak close to the clam, Raven began to whisper, "I am Raven. I have freed you from your prison in the sand and will happily return you to your home in the ocean, but first you must open your mouth and let me see what is inside."

The clam grumbled and opened its mouth no wider than the thickness of kelp. "I can fend for myself. You shall not get inside to take what is mine," replied the clam before its mouth closed.

"My friend, you will starve and dry out on the beach. Is your life worth what lies within your belly?" asked Raven.

The clam's mouth remained shut for sometime before once again opening to speak. "You are hard to argue with, Raven. Keep your word to return me to the ocean, and you may see what lies within."

"I promise," said Raven.

Slowly the mouth of the clam opened. Peering inside the cavernous belly of the beast, Raven spotted a group of strange creatures cowering together in a dark corner. He had never seen creatures like these before and knew they might be the ones to relieve him of his boredom. But the little beings were so afraid of him that they would not budge from the safety of the clam's shell.

But Raven was not about to give up on this opportunity. He began whispering sweet cajoling words to the creatures, enticing them out inch by inch with promises that were difficult to resist.

He told them of the world outside, filled with beauty and wonder. He spoke of all the glorious tastes and pleasures that could be had if they would only make the decision to step out into the sun. It took some time and all of Raven's powers of persuasion, but finally the creatures stepped out into the light of day.

And what odd-looking creatures they were. They had no fur or feathers, except for a nest of long black hair on top of round heads. Delicate skin covered their bodies, and instead of wings or claws, these creatures moved about on two skinny trunks and had two gangly appendages on their sides that were constantly fluttering around in a panic.

These were the first humans—the Haida people. They poured out from the mouth of the clam and onto the beach. When all the creatures had come out, Raven picked up the giant clam with his talons and flung it far out into the ocean as he had promised.

For the next several hours, Raven watched the curious creatures as they wandered about on the beach and into the edges of the forest, picking up everything they found and tasting all the food they could eat. The creatures amused Raven because they were a bit like him, curious and hungry, but after hours of watching them, he began to get bored. The "humans," as he called them, were busy with their own affairs and paid no attention to Raven.

Raven was about to fly off in search of other entertainment when he noticed something strange about the humans. He looked at every one of the creatures and could find no females.

Raven then had an idea. Wading out into the ocean, he collected as many mollusks as he could find. Although the mollusks had a hard outer shell, they had wonderfully soft, lipped underbellies. Putting his idea to the test, Raven tossed one of the mollusks onto the groin area of one of the men.

The mollusk adhered to the man's groin and instantly a wave of new emotions overcame him. While inside the clam, the man had never experienced such feelings of excitement. Blood rushed into his head and he began to writhe and squirm in the most humorous manner, and Raven was unsure whether the man was exhibiting pleasure or pain. Then suddenly a wave of energy passed through the man followed by a sudden, all-encompassing calm. The mollusk then dropped off and returned to its place in the shallows of the ocean.

Raven threw the other mollusks on at the men and each one found its target precisely. Once the men had released their torrent of energy, all the mollusks fell off and returned to the ocean. As the men recovered from this new experience and walked up and down the beach in a daze, Raven rolled on the ground with laughter. After a few minutes, the men composed themselves and continued to carry on with their curious ways.

Meanwhile, the mollusks back in their home were undergoing a transformation. Under the warmth of the sun and the changing of the tides, the mollusks grew and grew until their shells were ready to burst apart. One day, a huge wave crashed over top of the shells and broke them apart, washing the pieces onto the shore. When the waters receded, a group of brown-skinned women with black hair were laying on shore. Raven looked at the beautiful women and told them where they might find the men and what they might do with them. Raven now had something that would amuse him and people who could be made to revere him. He was truly happy, for the moment.

As for the humans, the women found the men and paired off, each group going their separate ways into the world. They built great homes and children soon followed, and within a few generations, the first tribes of peoples walked the earth.

No one knows what happened to all of Raven's children who were born on the beach that day, but they have survived because humans are still here on earth, with Raven watching over us as we live, love, make war and go about our rituals and complex lives.

Cast Down from the Spirit World

BEFORE THE TIME OF THE first peoples and long before the Great Flood, the Creator ruled in the sky kingdom. Far down below the clouds, there existed a vast world of water.

Raven lived in the sky world and served as the Creator's servant. But Raven did not do his job well, and one day he made the Creator angry and was cast out of the sky kingdom to the ocean world below.

Raven had mighty wings, but after flying back and forth over the sea for many days and nights, he began to tire. He looked everywhere in this world of water for a place to rest his weary wings, but he could not find even the smallest of islands.

Raven was about to fall out of the sky when he had an idea.

He began to beat his wings with so much force that it created hurricane-force winds that caused the waters to boil. Raven pushed so much water into the air with his powerful wings that they became the clouds. He left behind a clear path of rocks and sand that created a series of islands for as far as the eye could see. Raven finally rested his tired wings on one of the islands.

Raven lived on the island for many moons, and while he reigned over this kingdom, the barren islands began to grow trees and grasses. However, after investigating every part of the islands, Raven began to feel a little lonely. Life on the island was quiet and dull, and although Raven could eat as much as he wanted and sleep the days away, he had never felt more alone. Despite having been cast out of the sky kingdom, Raven decided to visit his old home among the clouds.

He gathered up some supplies, and the next morning he departed his island kingdom. He ascended into the sky past the first layer of clouds. He climbed so high into the sky that he could barely see the islands he had created down below. When he reached the top of the sky, he cut open a hole and found a great wall surrounding a village. The village was bathed in a glowing light. Raven knew this to be the home of the Chief of Light. Because everyone knew that the Creator had thrown Raven out of the sky kingdom, he decided to transform himself into the form of Eagle, because everyone respected Eagle.

Raven walked about the kingdom of the Chief of Light and admired its beauty. The chief had created the village in a beautiful valley with a brilliant river running through it. Raven, in the form of Eagle, saw that the Chief of Light had created the moon and its companion stars in the sky. The beauty of the kingdom was something to behold, and Raven coveted it greatly. After walking through the kingdom, he slept all night and awoke to a glorious ray of light from a great sun like he had never before seen. Raven thought, "If only I could have that on earth."

Raven wandered into the village and asked to be brought before the Chief of Light. The chief took a liking to the handsome Eagle and invited him in as a guest. For the next five years, Raven-as-Eagle lived with the chief and his five sons and became good friends with the eldest son.

One day, while searching for food with the chief's eldest son, Raven decided it was time to return to the lower world. Using kind words and false promises, he convinced the chief's son to take him to the place where the sun lived. The chief's son was powerless to resist and guided Raven, in the form of Eagle, to where the sun was kept.

When they reached the sun, Raven took a stick and lit in on fire by placing it in the sun. He then grabbed the sun with his other talons and flew high into the air. The chief's eldest son realized he had been tricked and ran back to his father's home. He told the chief that Eagle had stolen fire and the sun. At first, the father didn't believe his son because Eagle's character was thought to be without reproach. But when the father and son went outside, they saw Eagle flying quickly away.

"There's Eagle!" said the chief. "He's holding the sun in one talon and has taken fire in the other."

Raven flew with haste to the hole he had cut in the sky and dove down into the world he had once been banished from. The Chief of Light did not allow his people to follow the thief into the lower world because he did not want to cause a war and risk losing any of them.

Now transformed back to his original form, Raven flew off to the horizon and tossed the sun into the sky where it now sits and brings light during the day. Then Raven visited the first peoples and gave them the gift of fire, which they used to cook their food and heat their homes. It is because of Raven's deceit in the sky kingdom that the people on earth have the sun and the gift of fire.

The Lonely Sun

BEFORE THE CREATION OF the earth, the people and all livings things, there was nothing in the great universe except for the sun. The sun existed in this way for a long time, shining his light out into the vast darkness. The sun was content to live this way for many years. Yet with nothing to shine his light upon, he soon grew tired of being alone.

The sun took off a fiery piece of himself, formed it into a sphere and cast it out into the darkness, thus creating the earth. He used small pieces of the earth to form the bodies of men and women and spread them out all across the land.

The sun watched as the people raised children and lived out their lives. However, the sun had not taught the people how to live in peace, and soon they descended into wicked ways. The sun could do nothing but watch as friends turned against each other, families were torn apart and villages went to war. Many people died, and the ones who survived were living in misery.

The sun looked down upon his creation and wept tears of grief. For several years, the sun cried at the suffering of the people. He cried so much that his tears filled the rivers, lakes and oceans until the world was covered by water. The remaining people on earth tried to save themselves by climbing tall trees and mountains, but the waters reached high above, flooding everything.

All the people were caught in the floods and perished under the waters, except for one man and one woman, who were not consumed by wickedness and who survived by building a canoe. The sun saw that they were good people and finally stopped crying. It was this kind-hearted man and woman who began to repopulate the earth. The sun was no longer alone.

The Sun and Moon

IN THE DAYS BEFORE THE Great Flood, daylight did not exist. The world was as black as the deepest cave and only Chief To'ta and his people lived there, in a small village along a river that is now called the Thompson.

Chief To'ta had two sons and a daughter, all of whom had reached young adulthood. Rising Dawn was the eldest son, and High Walker was the younger son. Chief To'ta's youngest daughter was named Giver of Care.

After many years of living in the dark, Rising Dawn finally grew tired of fumbling about in the dark. He talked to his sister, and together they resolved to do something about their situation.

"Do you remember the stories Father once told to us as children about a time when the light shined down upon the land from up high, people walked about in happiness, and they could grow food and hunt with relative ease?" asked Rising Dawn.

"Of course I remember, but Father never saw the light of the sun and neither did grandfather before him. What makes you think we could do something about it?" said Giver of Care.

"The stories told of a place where the light went to sleep when the day was done," replied her brother. "It's a land far out in the east. Let's travel there and see what we might discover. We'll gather some wood and head out immediately."

When they had found enough wood, Rising Dawn fashioned a mask from the wood and he and his sister headed east. They walked for several days until they came upon an opening in the side of a mountain. They entered the cave and noticed a faint light far, far, down inside. Excited, Rising Dawn and Giver of Care ran toward the light. They arrived at a large wall in which one small point a ray of light shined through. They had discovered the resting place of the sun.

Careful not to get in front of the light, Rising Dawn took the mask out of his pack and gently placed an edge of the mask into the beam, setting it immediately ablaze. Rising Dawn and his sister started running back toward the west with the burning mask of fire lighting their way.

As they got closer to their home, the light from the fire attracted everyone in the village. Although the sudden appearance of light confused them, they were also happy that they could see.

However, the mask eventually burnt out, and the people were once again surrounded by darkness.

A council meeting was held to discuss the new discovery and to decide how to proceed. The eldest among them approached Chief To'ta with a message. "We are so happy that the light has returned and allowed us to see the faces of our loved ones, but Rising Dawn ran too quickly from the east. If he were to run a little slower, the light might last longer."

Chief To'ta took this message to his youngest son and asked him to venture to the east to bring back the light for the people.

"Father, although I run slower than my brother, the wood will burn my face before I reach home, and even if I make it back before then, the village will have less time in the light," said High Walker.

"Then, my son, build a thicker mask to hold the fire so that you might carry it without worry of being burned," replied Chief To'ta.

High Walker did so and travelled out to the east to greet the sun. After several days, the people of the village saw a faint light on the eastern horizon. High Walker was returning with the light from the sun. But the people again held council when the fire died, and they complained to the chief that his son had run too fast.

The wise chief thought long and hard about how he might please his people and finally came up with a solution. "Daughter, I want you to go with High Walker every day and hold him back when he starts to run too fast."

The next day, Giver of Care and her brother left on their journey to the east. When they had retrieved the light and were about halfway to the village, High Walker began to run too fast but Giver of Care managed to hold him back. The people of the village were content with this solution, and every day Giver of Care made sure High Walker stopped about halfway between the east and the west.

The tribe was pleased with High Walker. They brought him many gifts and gave the chief much praise for raising such a wonderful intelligent son. Rising Dawn, however, was not happy. People called him a good-for-nothing and laughed at him for failing where his younger brother had succeeded. This treatment angered Rising Dawn and he resolved to do something about it.

That night, he crept into his younger brother's room while he was sleeping. High Walker was lying on the floor with his mask on, and his breath blew sparks and smoke from the charred mask up through the chimney. The sparks rose into the sky where the embers became the stars in the sky and the smoke became the clouds. Rising Dawn took some of the white ash from the burning mask and painted his face with it.

Rising Dawn ran to his best friend's house while it was still dark and woke him from his slumber. "When you see me rise into the night sky, you must shout at the top of your lungs 'Hey! Everyone look into the sky! Rising Dawn has illuminated the night!'"

His friend did as he was told, and all the people came out of their homes and saw the glowing white face of Rising Dawn in the night sky. The people of the village began to cheer. From that night onward, Rising Dawn was known as the moon, and his brother took the name of the sun.

Since that time, the sun has provided for the crops, given warmth to the people and allowed them to see and enjoy the beauty of the world they inhabited. The moon controlled the movements of the tides, and when he fully appeared in the evening sky, his light gave the people comfort through the darkness of night.

Aientsik

LONG AGO, BEFORE THE EARTH as we know it existed, He Who Holds Up the Sky lived with his beautiful wife Aientsik in the sky kingdom. When she became pregnant, he took her to the Tree of Standing Light, uprooted the tree and pushed her through the empty black hole in the ground. Below Aientsik was a universe of water, nothing like the beauty of the world in which she had lived.

The animals from this universe of the water saw her failing out of their sky, but because of the blue colour of the skies, none of them were certain whether she was failing from the sky or coming up from the bottom of the lake. All the water animals began to argue about where she was coming from. The otter said that she was coming up from the bottom, and the beaver agreed. But the geese and the ducks could see that she was indeed falling from the sky. Without any further argument, the birds flew up and broke the fall of Aientsik, letting her rest on their backs. Gently, they drifted down to the surface of the water.

As soon as they landed on the water, a great turtle emerged from below and agreed to be the resting place of Aientsik. To make the back of the turtle more comfortable for Aientsik, the beaver dove into the water to try to gather some earth, but he could not hold his breath long enough to reach the bottom. Then the otter tried, but he too failed. The muskrat was the last one to make the attempt, and he succeeded. He placed the mud on the back of the turtle, and Aientsik laid down to rest.

When she woke the next day, she saw that the earth the muskrat had brought up from the waters had grown into a huge island and that her animal friends had made her a meal of corn soup, beans and squash. When she went to sleep and woke the next morning, she noticed that the earth had grown in size and that she was again provided with a meal of corn soup, beans and squash. Sometime later, Aientsik gave birth to the first peoples, and she raised them on corn soup, beans and squash. This is why corn, beans and squash are known as the three sister providers of the first peoples, the Mohawk.

The Coming of Humanity

LONG AGO, THE EARTH WAS different than it is now. The land was bare and there were no trees—only a few small bushes and little grasses. There were also no fish in the rivers or lakes. The people who lived during this time were called speta'kl. They were neither human nor animal but a mix of both. Gifted with powerful magic, the speta'kl could survive in a world where other people could not. Among them were many evil spirits, cannibals and monsters.

After many millennia of living in this world by themselves, the speta'kl were joined on earth when the Great Spirit, or Old Man, created the first peoples.

The first peoples did not have powers like the speta'kl and lived in fear of the evil forces in the world. To aid the people and protect them from evil, Old Man sent Coyote to rid the world of the evil spirits and monsters. Gradually Coyote defeated the evil speta'kl and transformed them into birds, fish, animals and trees. Coyote then made all the good speta'kl disappear. No one knows where they reside, but some say it is in the sky kingdom alongside the great Creator.

With all evil forces defeated, Coyote instructed the people on how to survive. He taught them how to hunt, how to built a canoe, how to grow vegetables and grain and many other things that the people could not live without.

When Coyote finished putting the world in order, he disappeared, leaving behind a beautiful peaceful place for the first peoples to live in and prosper. But Coyote was not always careful and was often lazy, and when he departed, he hadn't completely rid the earth of all things harmful. Somewhere on earth, under some rocks or in a cave, an evil spirit evaded Coyote and soon made its way back into the world.

Old Man travelled over the lands and could see that the evil that had been left behind in the world was now infecting some of the first peoples. Fighting and discord were spreading through villages as brothers turned on brothers and husbands killed their wives.

The state of the world made Old Man angry, so he gathered these people together and changed many of them into birds and fish and spread them through all parts of the world. Old Man took the good people and settled them in different places.

When Old Man departed from the earth, he left the lands as we see them today. All the animals and trees that you see were once the evil people of the earth, and the first peoples of the world are the descendants of the good people who were left on the earth by Old Man.

Silver Fox and Coyote Whittle Humanity

LONG AGO BEFORE OUR ancestors walked the earth, Silver Fox and his brother Coyote lived in the same home. They had been together since the dawn of time and were beginning to get bored of each other. Silver Fox decided to do something about it. He gathered some berry branches and whittled them down, working on his project all night. He planned to turn the leftover wood shavings into the common people, whereas the finished sticks would be warriors and chiefs.

As the sun broke over the horizon the next morning, Silver Fox was ready to bring his project to life. In the morning sun, he brought the first peoples to life. Silver Fox sent the people away, some in one direction and some in another. He and Coyote then sat down to a big feast.

Coyote was happy for his brother but a little jealous, as was his nature. So Coyote tried to emulate everything he had seen his brother do. He gathered some berry branches and worked all night whittling them down. Around sunrise the next day, everything worked perfectly, and the branches turned into men and women. But right away, Coyote, with lust in his eyes, began chasing after the women. After a long chase, he finally caught up with one of the women, but as soon as he touched the woman, she turned into wood shavings.

Ever since that time, it is said that if you are touched by the lustful Coyote, you will turn into wood shavings.

Inuit Origin of the Sun, Moon and Stars

AT A TIME WHEN DARKNESS covered the earth, a beautiful girl was visited while she slept by someone whose identity she could not discover. This person took advantage of the darkness and fondled the girl, then ran away.

The girl was determined to discover who the criminal was, so one night she painted her body with oil and soot. The next morning, as the family gathered around the fire, she discovered to her horror that her brother had black soot all over his hands. She scolded her brother and he tried to deny that it was him, but the proof was all over his hands. The father and mother were shocked by their son's actions, yelling and beating him every chance they could.

No longer able to take the abuse, the boy fled their home. The girl took a burning stick from the fire and ran after him. He tried to run away from her, but she was too quick. The boy took to the sky to escape, but his sister followed him. In the air, the boy changed into the moon, and the girl became the sun. The sparks that flew from the burning stick every time she poked him became the stars.

When you look into the sky, the sun is constantly in pursuit of the moon, which tries to keep in the darkness to avoid being discovered. When an eclipse occurs, it is said that the girl has caught her brother and has poked him with her stick, but he always escapes, only for the chase to begin again.

Creation and Death

A LONG TIME AGO, WHEN the world was not as we know it today, Old Man was travelling about the lands. As Old Man walked the barren lands, he created the mountains and the prairies and filled the lakes and rivers. Many of the things Old Man created were strange and seemed to have no purpose, but he was an old man after all, and he had many of his own ideas.

First, he made the mountains then descended to the land below where he pulled up the trees and the brush to make the prairies. As he moved north, when he got thirsty, he made a river; if he needed a bath, he created a lake; and if he needed shelter, he made trees. The world was thus created in this piecemeal manner.

But Old Man did more than just make mountains, rivers and lakes. He created all the animals to roam the lands. In the mountains, he made the deer out of dirt and turned them loose on the steep slopes and rocky cliffs. He quickly realized that this would not do because the beasts slipped and fell down the mountainside. Old Man then took the deer and placed them on the prairies, where they ran fast and full of grace. Old Man decreed, "Here you all shall roam."

On the prairies, Old Man created big horn sheep. The creatures did not travel well on the soft ground and looked out of place. So Old Man took the big horn sheep up into the mountains, where he let them roam free. The sheep skipped over the rocks and went up into the steep hills with relative ease. "This is what you were made to do, and you shall live here," said Old Man.

As Old Man walked along, he created bears, foxes and beavers, then he made eagles and hawks and all the other birds. When Old Man was done, he rested. Then one day, Old Man decided that he would make a woman and a child. He took up a ball of clay in his hands and moulded the shapes of two human beings. As the forms hardened, Old Man went out to create more of the world.

When he returned home the next day, he checked the clay shapes and saw that they were not ready.

On the second day, the shapes had begun to harden but were not quite ready. On the third day, the clay forms had hardened, and Old Man told the shapes to rise and walk. The shapes were suddenly filled with life and colour and began to move about. The child followed the woman down to the river. There, the woman asked Old Man, "Will we live forever?"

Old Man thought about her question. "We will decide this way. Pick up anything you see around you and throw it into the river. If it floats, when people die they will come back after three days, but if it sinks, death is the end," said Old Man.

The woman smiled. She looked around for something to throw. She selected a small round stone and tossed it into the river. The stone instantly sank to the bottom. "It is decided," said Old Man. "Life for your people will have an end."

One year later, the woman's child died. The woman went to Old Man and begged him to change the rule of death.

"The laws cannot be changed," said Old Man. "What I have decreed will forever be for humanity. Children, women, men and the greatest of chiefs are all the same and all must come to the end."

This is how the world came to be. It is Old Man who created it this way.

The Earth Turned Over

THE UNIVERSE WAS AT one time empty. Nothing existed. No light, no air, no earth and no people. Only the Creator existed. Then Creator made the earth, he created the mountains and the seas, he pushed the trees and the grasses up from the dirt, placed the animals all over the world and gave life to the first peoples.

After creating the universe and everything in it, the Creator said to the spirit Crane Wisakedjak, "I have created the perfect world. I leave the people of the world to you. You must teach them how to live. Show them all the things that will do them harm and show them all the things that will do them good."

These were the Creator's commands, but Wisakedjak paid no attention to his lord. Without guidance and wisdom, the people of the world began to fight and were filled with hatred. The world that was once perfect in every manner turned twisted and bloody. Friends turned on friends, loved ones killed each other over minor squabbles and humankind fought with the animals over territory. Wisakedjak was amused by the state of the world, but the great Creator was most displeased.

"Simple being!" screamed Creator to Wisakedjak. "Do you not see what you have done?"

"I don't understand, oh great Creator. If you created all this out of nothing, would it not be as easy to fix it all again?"

"I gave you a specific order and you disobeyed. If you do not keep the lands clean and free of hatred, I will take everything away from you and you will roam for eternity in misery," warned the Creator.

Wisakedjak promised the Creator he would take care of the world and his children, but one must never take the word of a trickster. Wisakedjak wanted to obey the Creator, but disobeying him was so much more fun. Instead of teaching the first peoples to live on earth in balance with nature, Wisakedjak taught them deceit and showed them all his tricks. He tricked the animals and the people for pleasure and made the animals hate the people and the people hate the animals. The hatred between the two groups led to many wars all over the earth—so much so that the rivers flowed red with blood and the dirt became stained with the spirits of millions of the Creator's creatures.

When the Creator observed what Wisakedjak had allowed to happen to his paradise, he became angry and shook the earth with his screams." You treat my creations as toys, so I will take everything away from you and I will wipe the face of the earth clean of this disaster."

Wisakedjak scoffed at the Creator's threats and returned to earth to play with his creatures. But after several days, the rains came and did not stop. Soon the rivers began to swell, but the rain continued to fall. Day and night, the rains continued. The rivers began to crest and the lakes swelled beyond their shores, and still the rain kept falling, harder and harder. Great winds lashed over the lands, causing the seas to boil. The rains finally caused the lakes to spill over and the rivers to break their banks. And once the seas came up, all the lands were submerged in water.

The people on earth were swept up in the great torrent and drowned. The birds were knocked from the sky and died. All the animals in the world were killed by the storm except for one beaver, one otter and one muskrat. Wisakedjak tried to stop the floods by using his magic, but the Creator's will was law and could not be broken.

With nowhere to rest, Wisakedjak sat down on the waters and added his tears to the torrent. Beaver, Otter and Muskrat heard him weeping and joined him in sorrow. Wisakedjak did not dare to call out for the Creator after making him so angry. Floating for days in a world filled with water, Wisakedjak yearned for the time before the chaos, when the old world was full of peace. But his selfishness had destroyed it all.

After days of misery and loathing, Wisakedjak spoke to Beaver, Otter and Muskrat. "We can once again live on land. I don't have the powers of the Creator, but if I were to have a bit of mud from the old earth beneath these waves, I might be able to build a small piece of land on which to live."

The crafty crane could not remake the earth as the Creator had done, but his powers could be used to create a small island. The only problem for Wisakedjak was that he could not dive down through the depths to retrieve a piece of the old earth. So instead of risking his own life, he turned to Beaver, Otter and Muskrat for help.

"My friends, the future is dim. If we do not bring up a piece of the old earth from beneath the waters, we will surely drown. Since I am the one who will create the new island, I can't be expected to dive down into the depths. If one of you will get the dirt for me, I will reward you handsomely," said Wisakedjak.

He then turned to Beaver and said, "You're a powerful swimmer and have excellent strength. If you go to the bottom and bring up the old earth, I will see to it that you have plenty of trees to build your new home so you will be comfortable in the winter."

Beaver agreed and took a deep breath then dove beneath the surface, descending into the dark abyss. Wisakedjak waited for any sign of Beaver but he was nowhere to be seen. Finally some bubbles broke the surface and Beaver emerged nearly dead from exhaustion. Despite his best efforts, Beaver returned empty handed.

"You must try again, noble Beaver. If you come back with the old earth, I will reward you with the most beautiful wife and she will give you many children," promised Wisakedjak.

After resting for a few moments, Beaver dove down into the dark waters but again returned with nothing to show for his efforts. Beaver tried a third time, but he was too tired.

"Hang your head in shame, Beaver!" screamed Wisakedjak. "I thought out of the three of you, you would succeed. You're a coward and shall get no favours from me."

Wisakedjak then turned to Otter. "It's your turn, noble Otter," said Wisakedjak, trying to flatter him. "You're sleek and light. You can move through the water much faster than Beaver could ever hope. Go now and bring me some of the old earth and I will reward you with the biggest, juiciest fish to eat."

Otter liked the sound of this offer. Twice he dove beneath the depths, but each time he surfaced with his hands empty.

"Dive once more and I will make you a wife," said Wisakedjak. Otter searched below the surface for what felt likes hours, but when he surfaced, again his hands were bare. "It's impossible," gasped Otter. "It is just too deep."

Wisakedjak's heart sank in despair. With only weak Muskrat left, Wisakedjak was sure he was never going to be able to rest his feet on dry land again. With nothing left to lose, he turned to little Muskrat. "Oh, brave and strong Muskrat," he said without feeling. "Although you are the smallest of the three, you will surely succeed. If you bring me a piece of the old earth, I will reward you with all the roots and grasses you can eat, and I will make sure you have the most secure and well-built home."

Muskrat jumped into the air and went head first into the water. He dove down for what seemed like an eternity but failed to reach the bottom before the need for air forced him back to the surface. But he was not about to give up and lose all the things Wisakedjak had promised him. After resting for a few minutes, Muskrat went back under the waves. He stayed under the water for much longer this time, and when he surfaced, his paws were caked in mud.

"You have done it, little one!" screamed Wisaked-jak. But Wisakedjak was greedy and he wanted more. "I will give you all the roots and grasses you can eat if you go back down and bring me some more of the old earth, and I will also make you a wife."

This time, Muskrat stayed down for so long that they all feared he had drowned in his efforts. They peered down into the waters looking for some sign of life, but nothing could be seen through the dark veil. Just when they were about to lose all hope, a few air bubbles broke the surface of the water. Beaver went to investigate and came back holding Muskrat. Although he was close to death, Muskrat was holding on tight to a large piece of the old earth.

Wisakedjak greedily snatched the earth from the exhausted Muskrat and used his magic to expand it into a small island. Wisakedjak, Muskrat, Otter and Beaver rested on the island and finally breathed a sigh of relief that they had not drowned in the great deluge of water.

Creator had already made life miserable for Wisakedjak, but he was not finished. "You have survived the Great Flood, but I also promised to take away your powers," the Creator's voice boomed from above. "You shall no longer have power over people and the animal world to force them to bend to your will. All I leave you with is the power of the tongue and deception."

The Creator then rebuilt the world as it was before. He made the rivers and the seas recede, he pulled the trees and the grasses out from the dirt and he put all the animals back into their environments. Then he moulded the first peoples out of the mud.

That is how the world was first created, then destroyed, and then reborn again.

Innocence Lost

IN THE TIME BEFORE PEOPLE roamed the earth, the animals, birds and fish all lived in peace along the gentle shores of Great Slave Lake. It was an idyllic place with temperate weather and an abundance of plants, leaves and berries for the animals to graze upon. No bears or wolves roamed the lands, so all the animals could enjoy their lives without fear or worry. This time of peace lasted for many generations, but all things have an ending.

One night, as the sun began to fade from the sky and the animals were preparing to go to their beds, a great darkness began to spread across the land. But this was a darkness like no one had ever before seen. The strange darkness inched its way across the sky, swallowing all light under its shroud.

The animals dismissed it as nothing to worry about and simply went to bed that night as they normally did. But as the darkness deepened overnight, it swallowed the moon and left the stars wrapped in black. As the world slept, thick snow began to fall, and it fell through the night.

When the animals awoke, they walked out of their homes and burrows not to find the warm morning sun, but the same dark skies and their lands blanketed in snow. The animals returned to their homes, but they could not escape the frigid temperatures. The snow became deeper and deeper with each passing day, and the sun could not penetrate the dark skies.

The animals began to suffer as their food supply lay buried beneath layers of heavy white snow. Many of them died of starvation. When there seemed to be no hope, White Bear, chief of the animals, finally called together a council.

"We are dying and we must figure out what to do!" yelled out Mouse.

"The people of the sky kingdom must surely know what is going on," suggested Beaver.

After hearing from the remaining animals, the chief made a decision. "We will send a group of messengers up into the sky kingdom and ask their people where the sun and the stars have gone."

So the chief, the birds and a team of the healthiest creatures flew up into the sky. They travelled through the darkness and the driving snow until finally they arrived at the main gates leading into the sky kingdom.

Once they passed through the main gates, they immediately found themselves in front of the home of the wolf clan. The house was made up of the skins and antlers of deer. There were no wolves on earth at that time, and the sight of so many dead deer scared the peace-loving animals of the earth. Despite their fear, the animals entered the home of the wolf and came upon four little wolf pups.

"Who are you?" cried one of the pups.

"It does not matter. Where is your father?" asked White Bear.

"He is out hunting caribou and will return shortly," said one of the wolf pups. "You better leave or else when he returns he will make you regret your trespassing."

The animals did not like the idea of having to meet the wolf pups' father. They quickly searched the room for anything that could help them back on earth. The only thing they saw were a few ornate boxes in the corner of the room.

"What's in those boxes?" one of the animals asked the pups.

"We can't tell you. Father told us to guard them until he returns from the hunt," said one of the pups.

"They must have something to do with our plight down on earth. Any animal who willingly kills another animal must truly have evil in his heart," said White Bear. "We must see what's inside!"

After pressing the pups for more answers, they finally relented. White Bear lifted the lid of one of the boxes. Inside were the rains. He opened another and found the winds. He opened another that contained the moon and the stars. As he was about to open the last box, the father of the wolves announced his arrival with a long howl that echoed across the lake.

"You can't open that box!" screamed the pups.

The animals held a quick council and came up with a plan to save their skins from the anger of the wolf and to discover the contents of the last unopened box.

White Bear said, "Since the wolf returns from the hunt by canoe, I want Mouse to swim out to the boat and gnaw a hole in it. That way, he will sink to the bottom and perish. This will give us enough time to discover the contents of the final box and return home safe and alive."

Mouse did what he was told, and the wolf father's canoe sank to the bottom of the lake. Because he could not swim, the wolf drowned. When Mouse returned to the wolf's house, the chief finally opened the last box, and inside they found the sun. The chief gathered up the remaining boxes, and he and the rest of the animals ran toward the gates back to their world.

During this time, the young wolf pups had alerted the rest of the wolf clan and those of the black bear. They went after the intruders from the earth kingdom. Using their strong sense of smell, the wolf and black bear clans chased the animals to the gates. But they were too late.

The chief of the animals had already opened the boxes and tossed their contents down to earth where the rains, the winds, the moon, the stars and, most importantly, the sun returned. Quickly jumping on the birds, the chief and the other animals descended into their realm to find the snows had already begun to melt and the winds had brought back warmth to the air. But all was not well.

The damage caused by the heavy snows and the freezing cold had killed off most of the plants. The forests would need time to replenish. To make matters even worse, the wolf and the black bear clans from the sky kingdom had followed the animals back down to earth and now roamed freely. Being natural hunters, the wolves and bears began to kill many of the animals for food.

The animals were so hungry that they sent out Raven to look for food. He was the most beautiful and elegant of all birds at that time. His feathers were as white as the clouds and his features were beyond compare. While in the air, he happened upon an animal that had recently been killed by one of the wolves. Normally, Raven would have been sick at the sight of one of his dead clan members, but his hunger was too great. He landed on the ground next to the dead beast and began to feast on its flesh. By the time he had had his fill, his white feathers had turned black. As a result of Raven's gruesome act, certain animals learned to like the taste of other animals' flesh. This is why all animals dislike Raven.

Although the sun had returned to the lands, the peaceful life that had previously surrounded the animals was long gone. Raven had introduced the eating of flesh to some animals. Many of the animals chose not to eat flesh, but this only brought division among the different animals. Each animal moved to its own areas. The birds were safest in the sky and nesting in the trees, while the buffalo chose the plains filled with grass for them to eat. Because the animals no longer lived together, they quickly lost their original language and the ability to communicate with one another. That is why bears cannot speak with beavers, or eagles talk to ravens.

Before the Flood

Now WAS THE TIME before the flood.

Now was the time before the waters came.

There was nothing as we know it.

It was empty, for there was nothing.

Out of the nothing, there was an old being.

Out of nothing, the old being floated.

The old being was Old Man Raven.

And he was all alone in a world of nothing.

Alone, bouncing in an ocean of black.

Alone, adrift in a sea of nothing.

Old Man Raven drifted and drifted.

There was nothing but time to be lifted.

Now Old Man Raven found he had a voice.

Now Old Man Raven found he could speak.

He said to the water, "It is hard to be alone."

But the water said nothing, not even a tone.

Old Man Raven grew tired and weak.

Old Man Raven was listless and bored.

"Is there anyone out there?" he called. "I will not be ignored!"

Out of the dark he heard a call.

Out of the dark came two red-eyed loons.

Old Man Raven suspiciously looked them over.

The two red-eyed loons did the same to Raven.

Old Man Raven finally had someone to talk with.

Old Man Raven finally had someone to listen.

"Where did you come from?" asked Raven.

"We came from nowhere," came the reply.

"I too came out of nothing," replied Old Man Raven. "I too came out of thin air."

"Please tell me what you have seen," said Old Man Raven. "Is there more to this world than water?"

The loons looked at each other and shrugged.

"We have seen nothing, until we saw you. This world is empty. What should we do?"

The water sloshed beneath them.

The sky did not change colour.

Old Man Raven turned to the loons.

"Do you think there is more?" he asked.

"There is always more," answered the loons. "There is always more than what appears."

Old Man Raven looked up, to the left and then to the right.

"I see nothing but dark waters and air," he said.

"There is more under this water," chimed the loons. "There is more everywhere. You just need to look harder."

Old Man Raven's head darted about, his eyes wide open.

But again, nothing but water and darkness caught his eye.

"Under the waves is where you will find more. Under the waves is where things live," sang the loons.

And in a flash, one of the loons dove beneath the waves.

The other loon stayed above to watch and wait.

The air stayed quiet.

The air stayed still.

While Old Man Raven waited, he felt a sudden chill. "Do you think your friend is still alive?" he asked the loon. "Do you think your friend will live?"

"Fear not, for he is a wonderful swimmer. He can stay down for long and just might bring us dinner," said the loon.

Just as the loon spoke, the other loon broke through the water's surface.

The loon had returned with something in his beak.

It was hard, it was smooth and it was wet.

"There must be more down there, this I would bet," said Old Man Raven.

Down the other red-eyed loon went below the waves.

Down the loon went into the unknown.

Old Man Raven and the loon waited for the other loon to surface, hoping he did not go down without a purpose.

Again they waited for the loon to surface.

Again Raven worried that the loon might not make it.

But to his surprise, the red-eyed loon came back.

Only this time he held within his beak something black.

Old Man Raven looked it over and saw that it was mud.

Old Man Raven looked both treasures over and knew what could be done.

"We can make this something into more and it will change this place," said Old Man Raven to the loons.

He took the mud within his hand and placed it close to his face.

With a magical breath the mud grew and grew.

With a magical breath the mud expanded and created the lands.

But the lands were flat and boring.

"This is not a place for birds like us made for fun and for soaring," said one of the loons.

Old Man Raven took the round rock from the beak of the loon.

Old Man Raven blew on the rock and pieces flew from his hands.

Trees grew, grasses came up and flowers bloomed.

The red-eyed loons looked out over the lands and said, "It's too flat. It's too groomed."

Raven dragged his talons over the lands and pulled up mountains.

Raven dug his talons in deeper and created valleys.

The red-eyed loons cried and sang with delight.

However, Old Man Raven still felt alone and afraid.

"The world is too quiet and we need more. The world is too empty—I will fill it with life," he said.

He then gathered up more mud and made two forms.

Raven flapped his wings and the first peoples emerged from the storm.

The red-eyed loons cried, "We want some creatures like us! Can you fill the skies?"

Old Man Raven plucked some feathers from the loon's tail.

He blew on them, and all the birds of the world were created.

Old Man Raven looked out across the earth and was happy.

He had created the earth and everything on it.

One of the red-eyed loons then asked, "Is there more? Would you guess?"

"There is always more. Sometimes good, sometimes bad. Is there more to come? Yes."

Raven Finishes his Work

FROM THE BEGINNING OF TIME, Raven travelled all over the world doing many wonderful things as he went along. If he came to a village that was plagued by a monster, Raven slayed it so that the people could live in peace. If a village was overtaken by an evil spirit, Raven used his powerful magic to send it away.

When the all-knowing Creator made humanity, it was Raven who gave the people their names and taught them different languages. He taught the people how to hunt the deer, how to pull the fish from the river and how to grow food from the soil. Without Raven, the people would not have learned how to make a good lodge or know how to dress themselves in clothing. Raven liked to have fun, so he also showed the people how to make music and how to dance.

Sometimes Raven made mistakes or played mean tricks on the people because he was not perfect. One of his favourite pastimes was telling lies. Raven loved to make his stories sound more incredible than they were, especially if beautiful young women were around him to listen. One story he loved to tell was of the time he defeated the giant spider who dwelled high up in the mountains. He said he had saved thousands of people from its evil jaws by slaying it with a simple knife. However, in truth, the giant spider had killed itself when it fell over a cliff and splattered on the rocks below as it was chasing Raven away.

Another way Raven liked to get into trouble was by copying what someone else did. This is how he became known as the great imitator.

But there came a time when Raven had done everything he could think of doing, had travelled to every corner of the world and had most of his pleasures satisfied. For years he wandered about looking for something to do but could find nothing. The Creator saw Raven wandering about and said to himself, "Raven has done all I had asked of him. It's time I bring him back to where he began."

So the Creator came down to earth and transformed himself into an old man.

"Raven, I am the chief of all creation," said the old man to Raven. "I was the one who first sent you to earth to make things run properly."

"I don't believe you are the Creator of all things," replied Raven. "Prove your power."

So the old man looked over to a mountain and lifted it from the earth with a simple thought and then placed it back on its foundation.

"Oh, I see you are the Creator. What would you have of me?" asked Raven.

"Your work is finished here on earth. Now you will go where I have made a beautiful home for you," said the old man.

Raven then disappeared, and no one has seen him since or knows where he rests.

The Creator then told the people, "Raven and your Creator will not be seen again until the earth spirit is very old. When that time eventually comes, we will return. Raven will be seen first, and then I will appear with all the spirits of the dead. Together we will put an end to this universe and then begin again. This is my word. This is the way of life. Enjoy this world and live in peace."

Now the people await the return of Raven and the Creator.

Part II:
The Origins of the Natural World

Goddess of the Sea

LONG AGO, WHEN THE WORLD was new and few people were on earth, a man lived with his daughter Sedna on a solitary northern shore. The man's wife had passed on to the spirit world many years earlier, and the father and daughter now lived a quiet life.

Sedna grew into the most beautiful girl in all the lands. But she was vain and thought she was too beautiful to marry any suitor that came her way. Villages from far away had heard of her beauty and sent their most handsome and eligible young men to seek her hand in marriage, but no man could ever hope to meet her high standards. The young men would travel for days to see Sedna, but all of them returned to their villages with their heads down. Sedna never worried about finding a husband as she was too busy brushing her long black hair in the reflection in the water most days.

Finally one day, her aging father came to her and said, "Sedna, my daughter. We have no food. We will go hungry if you do not marry. You need a skilled hunter to take care of you and provide you with everything you need."

Sedna ignored her father and returned to brushing her hair.

Several days later, her father spotted another young hunter approaching their camp. The man was dressed in the most elegant of furs and appeared to be healthy despite having his face covered by a hood. The father said to him, "If you seek a wife, I have the most beautiful daughter. She can cook and sew, and I know she will make you happy."

Sedna's father led the man down to the water where she was still brushing her hair. She knew why the man had come, and before the young man could say anything, she told him to go back to where he came from.

"But, my lady, you have not heard my reasons," said the man in the most enticing of voices. "Come with me to my homeland where no one goes hungry. My tent is lined with the most luxurious skins, and you shall sleep under the softest bearskins. My people will bring you everything you desire and will worship your beauty. Your lamp will always be filled with oil and your pot filled with meat. So what is your answer, beautiful Sedna?"

Even though she could not see the stranger's face, his words and promises appealed to Sedna, and they wed immediately. Together, they travelled over the vast sea to the home of her spouse, and after the long and hard journey, she discovered that her spouse had shamefully deceived her.

Her new home was not built with beautiful pelts but was covered in rotting fish skins. The house was built from coarse rock and offered no protection from the wind and snow. Instead of soft bearskins for a bed, she had to lay on rough, wet walrus hides and had nothing to eat but small, disgusting fish.

On her first night in her new home, her husband came to lie with her. He finally pulled down his hood to reveal not a handsome young hunter but a gull in disguise. He laughed at her misery, saying, "Waaa, ahhh, ahhhh, ahhhh!" as gulls do, and Sedna cried and cried.

At night, she sang a woeful song to her father. "Oh Father, I am so wretched. If you knew, you would come to rescue me from this misery. I wasn't made to live with these foul birds. If you knew, you would come rescue me in your boat and we would hurry away over the waters back to our home and our quiet life. These gulls treat me as a stranger and give me miserable food meant for animals not people. Oh come, Father, and take me away!"

For over a year, Sedna cried every night, until one day, when the snow had melted, her father heard his daughter's cries carried on the arctic winds. He got into his kayak and travelled the great distance to see his daughter.

After a long and difficult journey, he arrived at the place where Sedna now lived. She greeted him with a great amount of joy and immediately asked him to take her back to their home while the gull was away hunting. She told him of the miseries she had to endure and the hardships she was exposed to while living with the gulls.

Her father vowed to seek revenge on the gull for the injustice done to his daughter. When the gull returned from hunting, the father killed the gull, took Sedna to his kayak, and they left the land that had brought her so much sorrow.

When the other gulls returned from their hunt and found their companion dead and his wife missing, they were angry. They immediately formed an army to seek out the murderers and exact vengeance upon them.

The gulls did not have to fly far before they spotted the kayak with Sedna and her father. Together, the gulls began to stir up the waters with the power of their mighty wings combined. The winds pushed up immense waves that threatened Sedna and her father with destruction. Some of the birds swooped down and attacked the pair, biting at their heads and hands to try to get them to fall overboard.

The father was terrified, and in an effort to save his own life, he threw Sedna into the raging waters, hoping it would appease the wrath of the gulls. Sedna managed to grab onto the edge of the kayak with a firm grip. Her suddenly cruel father took out his knife and cut off some of her fingers. They fell into the sea, and while sinking to the bottom, the fingers transformed into seals.

Although injured, Sedna was able to hold onto the kayak. Now in a panic, her father cut off her other fingers, and they sank to the bottom of the water and transformed into whales. Sedna became weary from the struggle and could no longer hang onto the kayak. She began to sink to the bottom of the ocean herself.

Sedna was sinking to a certain death, but her rage kept her from drowning. She became the goddess of the sea. She lies beneath the waves with her companions, the seals and whales.

When Sedna is angry, she drums up violent seas and heavy storms. Hunters must treat her with respect and pay homage to her. Shamans from the world above must dive deep down into the waters to comb her long black hair. This gesture calms her fury, and when she is calm, she releases the mammals to allow the Inuit to hunt.

This is the legend of Sedna, goddess of the sea.

The Storyteller

A BABY BOY WAS ONLY A few weeks old when both his mother and father died. The boy was placed in the care of his mean aunt, who never let him play or have any fun at all as he was growing up. His days were spent doing chores around the house and tending to his aunt's every need. The boy did his chores, but if his aunt was not watching, he would often drift off and daydream about playing with the other children and what life might be like outside the village.

It was for this reason that she gave him the name of Dreamer Boy.

Realizing that she could not keep the boy locked up in the village for the rest of his life, one day the aunt gave him a bow and some arrows and told him it was time to learn to hunt. She told him that he had to give back to the village what you take. The night before he was to set out on the hunt, he could not sleep. He was wondering about all the things he might see and do out in the lands beyond his village.

The next morning, Dreamer Boy's aunt woke him before sunrise, like she always did. After a breakfast of corn, the boy grabbed his bow and arrows and prepared to leave the village.

"I have packed some food for your journey. Now go out and bring back some game for the village. However, do not waste time. You are to hunt for game and return to the village. Nothing more. Understand?" said the aunt sternly.

Dreamer Boy did not pay any attention to his aunt's lecture. He said a quick goodbye and ran out of the village. For several hours, he wandered through the forest, staring up into the sky and taking in everything that surrounded him. He walked past lakes, saw beautiful waterfalls and caught sight of animals that he had seen hunters take back to the village.

After some time gazing at the world about him, Dreamer Boy finally set to work catching food for the village. He knew that if he hunted enough animals, he might be allowed to return to the forests, so he set to the hunt. When he had finished, he had killed more creatures than the best hunters in his village. Walking back to the village, he thought his aunt would surely be proud.

When he arrived at the village, he was greeted by his aunt, who was surprised at his success but happy. "You have done well Dreamer Boy. Each day you will go out hunting and try your best to bring home as much game as you can," she said.

The young man dutifully listened to his aunt and went to bed that night dreaming of the new things he might see tomorrow. He awoke the next morning before sunrise, ate breakfast and almost left before his aunt could give him some food rations for the day.

Again, Dreamer Boy started off into the woods. For several hours, like his previous trip, he simply wandered through the woods, over hills and through marshes, exploring the world around him. As a boy, he had never been told about the world outside the village. In fact, no one from his village knew much about the world—they only knew the lands that surrounded them.

After spending a full day in the forest, Dreamer Boy returned to his village with more birds than he had brought home on his last journey. Giving them to his aunt, she tied the birds in separate bundles and proudly handed them out to her neighbours.

"You see how he has become a good hunter," she said, pointing to her nephew with pride for the first time in his life. "I was so worried for his future, but he has proven himself."

For several days, Dreamer Boy started off each morning, venturing out deeper and deeper into the woods in search of adventure and animals for the village. On the seventh day of the hunt, he had walked so far that his feet began to ache. Looking for a place to rest, he saw a small hill. At the centre of the hill was a large oak tree. He walked up the hill and sat down against the trunk of the tree. While opening his pack, he was about to eat some of his rations when he heard a voice. "Do you want to hear some stories?"

Startled, the boy looked around but could see no one. He looked behind the tree, up in the branches but could not find the source of the mysterious voice.

"Do you wish to hear my stories?" exclaimed the voice again.

Rising to his feet, Dreamer Boy loaded his bow and began pointing it at random. "Who goes there? Show yourself or risk death by my skilled hands!" he threatened.

"I wish to tell you my stories," said the voice.

This time, Dreamer Boy finally realized that the voice was coming from the tree. "What is a story? What will you be telling me?" asked the boy.

"You have never heard a story before? A story is a recounting of past events that happened long, long ago," said the tree. "I will tell you a story if you give me the birds you have hunted."

Dreamer Boy was curious about these stories. He had never heard of a story in all his years growing up in the village, and he was sure none of the elders knew what they were either. Unable to put aside his curiosity, the young man gave the birds he had caught during the day to the tree. He sat back down and listened as the tree began to tell stories of a time long ago.

The tree recounted incredible tales of mystical giants and animals spirits that once roamed the lands. Dreamer Boy sat mesmerized as the tree recounted story after story until the sun began to fade from the sky.

"I have told you enough for today," said the tree. "Come tomorrow and I shall tell you more. But you must bring more game for me to eat, otherwise my stories will remain untold."

Dreamer Boy quickly ran back toward the village, hunting the few birds he saw along the way. When his aunt looked at his catch, she asked why he had caught so few animals when just the day before he had caught so many.

"I am sorry, Auntie, but I have hunted too well in the surrounding forests and have killed most animals in the area. Now I must travel farther to hunt," he replied.

The next day, Dreamer Boy awoke before the rise of the sun, grabbed his bow and arrow and his provisions and left the village. He wandered through the forest, thinking of all the magical stories the tree had told him the day earlier. Before he reached the spot where the tree resided, he shot and killed three birds.

When he arrived at the tree, Dreamer Boy called out, "I have brought you food. Now tell me more wonderful stories of the time long ago."

He sat down and listened as the tree recounted more incredible tales. The boy listened intently, trying to picture these incredible worlds that the tree spoke of. After several hours, the tree stopped telling his stories. "I am tired," he said. "Come to see me tomorrow and bring more food for me to eat and I will tell you more stories."

On his way back to the village, Dreamer Boy killed a few more birds and brought them home. His aunt was the first person to greet him.

"Why have you caught so few animals today?" she asked with a look of anger on her face. Dreamer Boy tried to explain again that he had been hunting so well that the forest had grown quiet, so he had to travel even farther to find any animals.

That night, as Dreamer Boy slept, his aunt went to her neighbour and spoke to her about her nephew's strange behaviour. "He brings home so few birds for us to eat when he used to bring us such a plentiful bounty. There is something strange going on," said the aunt.

The neighbour was equally suspicious of the boy's behaviour and excuses, so the next morning she sent her son into the forest to follow the boy and find out what Dreamer Boy was doing.

The neighbour's son followed at a distance and watched as Dreamer Boy killed several birds. Everything seemed normal until Dreamer Boy suddenly stopped hunting and began to run at a fast pace toward the west. The neighbour's boy could barely keep up with Dreamer Boy because he was running so fast. They eventually came to a clearing in the woods. Dreamer Boy ran up a small hill and sat down at the base of a large tree. The boy crept closer and suddenly heard Dreamer Boy talking to someone. He looked all around to see where the voice had come from but only saw Dreamer Boy.

"Who are you talking to?" asked the boy. "What are you doing here?"

Dreamer Boy turned quickly and said, "You scared me! I'm here to listen to stories."

"Stories? What are stories?" asked the boy.

"They are incredible tellings about things that happened long before you or your grandparents were born. Come sit with me a while and ask this tree, 'Can you tell me stories?'" said Dreamer Boy.

The neighbour's boy asked the tree the question and immediately it began to relate the most wonderful stories. The boys listened for hours until the sun descended on the horizon. Then the tree said, "Come by tomorrow with more food and I shall tell you more stories. Go now. I must rest."

On the way back to the village, the boys quickly killed as many game animals as they could. When they returned to their village, Dreamer Boy's aunt asked the neighbour's son why they had not caught many animals. He explained that he had followed Dreamer Boy for a while and then they hunted together. There were simply fewer animals left in the forest, he told her.

Not satisfied with this excuse, the aunt asked two of the village's best hunters to follow her nephew to figure out what was going on.

The next morning, Dreamer Boy left before sunrise and caught many animals along the way to the forest. Concealed, the two men from the village watched as Dreamer Boy ran to a small hill, placed his day's catch inside the hollow of a large tree and then sat down. The hunters thought it was strange behaviour. They were even more shocked when they saw him place his mouth to the tree and speak to it.

"I have come to hear more stories," said Dreamer Boy to the tree.

The two men were surprised when a voice answered the boy.

"What are you doing, Dreamer Boy? Who are you talking to?" one of the men demanded.

"I'm listening to stories told by the tree. Come sit nearby and listen," said the boy.

The two men sat down beside the boy and heard the strange voice tell the most wonderful stories. They sat and listened until it was almost night.

"Tomorrow, you will bring all the villagers here and I'll tell them my stories," said the tree. "Have everyone in the village bring me something to eat and I'll tell tales of unimaginable beauty and excitement."

Running back to the village, the boy gathered everyone in the village and told them of the tree and its incredible stories. The chief of the village ordered the people to gather up some food and head out to the tree upon first light the next morning. When dawn broke the next day, the people followed Dreamer Boy to the tree. When everyone had placed their food in the tree and sat down, the tree spoke.

"For years, I have sat in the forest and no one was able to hear my call until one day the little Dreamer Boy walked by and heard my voice call out to him. It is because of him that I now relate and entrust these stories to his people," said the tree. "I will tell you all the stories of long ago, when the world was not like it is today. The world of before was filled with powerful spirits of good and evil. You will now listen. But pay careful attention, for this will be the last time I repeat these stories. Remember them for they are what connects you to each other and to all those who have came before."

For the next seven days, the tree told the people story after story. They listened in amazement of the things it said and of the worlds that came before. On the seventh day, as the sun was fading from the sky, the tree stopped. "I have finished," it exclaimed. "Now remember everything I've told you. Pass these stories down to your children and great grandchildren. Tell them to your friends and give them to strangers. I know of everything that came before, and I've given you that knowledge so that you might understand the world better."

This is how the Seneca people know what happened in the world before this one. Some believe if the stories were not told and shared, the world would end.

Curious Brothers

NOT LONG AFTER THE CREATION of the world, three brothers roamed the frozen landscapes of the north. Life was difficult during the best times of the year, but in the midst of the cold season, life became even more of a struggle. Food was scarce, and to make matters worse, the sun disappeared for months on end.

No one knew where the sun went during the winter, not even the elders of the brothers' village. Being curious young men, one winter when the sun disappeared on the horizon, the brothers decided to follow it in hopes of learning where it went and to find out if there was another part of the world that did not look like their own. After gathering a few provisions from their home, the three brothers said goodbye to their parents and set off to explore the lands that none of their people had ever seen.

The brothers travelled through blinding snowstorms and freezing temperatures for what felt like weeks. Heading in a southwesterly direction, the brothers hoped that the sun might eventually cast a faint light over the horizon, but after countless hours trudging through the cold, the brothers were ready to give up their search. Their food rations were getting low and they had not seen any animals to hunt because the snow continually blinded them. Without enough food or strength to turn around and head back to their village, the brothers continued south.

When all hope seemed to have faded, the brothers noticed a dim light off in the distance radiating on the horizon. With a renewed sense of energy, the brothers headed toward the light. For three days and two nights, they walked through the snow until they reached the light's source, which was an enormous house made of ice whose walls emitted a beautiful blue light.

The brothers walked around the house until they came to the opening of the ice castle.

"I'll leave my pack here in case someone should come by. They will know we were here," said one of the brothers.

Now that the brothers were out of the blowing wind and snow, they cleared their eyes of ice and water and gazed upon a glorious open room that stretched far into an endless darkness. As they walked around the room, they saw that the ceiling of the great hall was so high that it could not be reached by the points of their arrows. The size of the room made the brothers wonder what kind of huge beast could have built this place. But they put aside their fears and continued on, their curiosity pushing them forward step by step.

For days, they travelled through the great hall and did not stumble upon its end. They managed to replenish their food stocks when they happened upon a group of deer and managed to kill two. Days turned into months, and the brothers continued on. They were weary on their journey but determined to find the place where the sun goes to rest. For years, they walked through the hall and found nothing. At last the brothers were so tired that they could only crawl through the darkness, but they were never going to give up their pursuit of an answer.

Two of the eldest brothers had grown old and grey and had to stop crawling. They could no longer continue on the journey to discover where the sun began and whether there was another part of the world unlike their own. They said their final goodbyes to their young brother and then died together in the great hall, having failed in their quest.

The youngest brother was more resolved than ever to succeed so that his brothers had not died in vain. He continued down the hall for several more days until he finally saw a light at the end of the hall. As he got closer, the light blinded his eyes, but he ran and burst through the entrance. Once his eyes became adjusted to the light, he looked around him and noticed his pack was in the same place that he had left it at the beginning of the journey. He had travelled for so long only to return to the same place where his story began.

Having found the answer to his quest, and now an old man, he returned to his village and told his people, "The sun has no home, and this earth is simply on a very large ice house."

How the People Got Fire

A LONG, LONG TIME AGO, when there were no matches or lighters, only one man in the world had the gift of fire. Even though the people of the world could not cook their meat and had no fire to warm themselves, the man just watched their misery and did nothing. He would not even let the people take a little bit of the fire on a stick.

Many of the people tried to take the fire from him by force, but the man was powerful and killed anyone who came near his fire. No one had the courage to challenge him despite their suffering.

Then one day, Deer said to the people, "Don't worry. We'll have fire to warm ourselves and to cook our food. I can run really fast. I'll use my speed to get fire from the evil man and will give some to everyone. I need all the people of the village to gather around the lodge of the man with the fire. You will all sing for him while I get the fire."

So the people of the village followed Deer down to the man's home and they all began to sing loudly. The man who had the fire came out of his lodge to listen to their song. Normally he would have killed them all, but the singing made him happy.

As the man gazed upon the people as they sang, Deer managed to slip through the crowd of people and quickly enter the man's lodge. Deer grabbed a stick from the fire, but he accidentally touched the hairs on his knees with the burning stick—this is why the hairs inside the deer's leg is black and smells of smoke.

Deer quietly left the man's home and slipped back through the crowd. He started to run as fast as he could back to the village. The man who had the fire saw Deer running away, but he could not catch him because Deer was too fast. In this way, Deer saved his people from a life of cold and misery.

The Birth of Song

LONG AGO, HARDLY ANY ANIMALS roamed the earth, and no birds flew in the skies. During this warm period that only lasted for six full moons, the children had nothing to play with except the trees. When the seventh moon came, the great White Bear of the North blew his cold winter breath across the land, and Howling Wolf's winds stripped the trees bare. The cold and the snows left the children with nothing with which to amuse themselves. Winter left the lands barren and forced them to stay inside.

The lack of animals was also a problem. When the children left the sweat lodge after the ritual fast, they could not see any animals from whom they could take a name. It was a custom for the children to take the name of the first animal or thing they saw when leaving the lodge.

The state of the world made all the children sad, and for many days they cried as the cold arctic breath of White Bear blew down on them. One day, a girl from a village spoke to the great Glooscap and asked him a favour.

"Mighty spirit Glooscap, who created the earth, the water, the sun and the stars, please fill the world with more animals and more life so that all the children might one day laugh and play again in wonder at your creation. We know winter must come and end our summer fun, but without animals around us, we will be nameless children."

Glooscap heard the girl's pleas. When White Bear retreated to his lands in the north and the flowers once again began to bloom, Glooscap gathered up all the fallen dead leaves and threw them into the air. Carried by the wind, the leaves transformed into all different kinds of birds. Perching in the trees, the birds began to sing and fill the air with the most beautiful music. The children were happy because they could finally find names for themselves and amuse themselves in the world.

The Challenge

IN THE EARLY YEARS OF EARTH'S existence, there was no war between people. All the tribes of the lands lived in peace. During this time, there lived a man who had the most beautiful daughter in the entire world. She was the object of many young men's affections, but every time an eligible bachelor asked for her hand in marriage, she always said no and told him she did not want to marry. Her refusal to marry made her parents upset.

"How come you will not marry?" asked her father. "Some of these young men are handsome and noble and are good hunters."

But the young woman did not listen to her father. She only shook her head and ran away from his questions.

A short time later came the annual dance. All the clans from the surrounding villages showed up in their best garments and wore their finest ornaments. The most handsome boys from all the clans were in attendance and so was the man's beautiful daughter, but she just stood in the corner, avoiding the boys and turning down their requests to dance. Several of the boys tried to ask for her hand in marriage, but to each one she said no. Her father became upset by her response and said, "Something is wrong with you! All the best men in all the villages have asked for your hand and you say no. You must be hiding something. You must have a secret lover!"

"You shame your family," added the girl's mother. "You play outside the bonds of marriage with a lover and might bring a child into this house without us even knowing the father!"

"Father! Mother!" pleaded the girl. "Please listen to me. I don't have a secret love. The god of the sun spoke to me long ago and told me never to marry. He said I was his and that I would be happy and live for many generations."

The girl's parents looked at each other and the father said, "If the god of the sun has told you this, then it shall be, and no one will ever question you again."

In the same village, a poor young man wandered alone. His father and mother had died when he was a child and he had been an orphan ever since. He had no home, no wife and no status in the village. He simply travelled about and lived day by day on the kindness of strangers and whatever food he could scrounge together. Despite being poor and dressed in old clothing, he was a handsome man, except for a large scar than ran from his eye down to his lower jaw. Neither the boy nor anyone in the village knew how he had received the distinctive mark across his face.

In the man's youth, the boys in the village had made fun of him, laughing and playing mean tricks on him. Even though he was now a young man, the villagers still made fun of him, giving him the nickname "Scarface." At dances, they teased him and dared him to ask the girl who was promised to the sun to marry him. He got tired of the taunting and told his tormentors, "Fine! I will ask her to marry me."

Scarface waited down by the river where the girl normally went to fetch water. When she arrived, he summoned up the courage to speak to her. "You are surely the most beautiful woman in all the world," he said to her. "All the young men in the village have asked for your hand and you have refused. I am poor. All my family has departed from this earth. I am alone and am disfigured by this scar. But I cannot live my life without knowing if you could love me, so I am standing here and asking you to be my wife."

The girl blushed and looked down at her feet. No other boy had been so honest with her before, and despite the mark on his face, he was truly the most handsome man she had ever seen.

"What you say is true. I have said no to all my suitors. They were rich and handsome, but they lacked courage. I will be your wife. You may be poor, but my father shall provide us with animals, and my mother shall sew new clothes for you. The people will be happy for us and they will celebrate," she said, jumping into his arms.

As the young man was about to kiss her, she stopped him. "Why do you stop me?" he asked.

"I can't marry you yet. I promised Sun I would not marry and that I belong to him. If I obey his rules, I shall be permanently happy and live for many generations in peace. But I now am in love with you. I want you to travel to Sun and tell him that you wish to marry me. Tell him that I have been his faithful servant and have never betrayed our bond. If you fail to find the sun, do not return to me because it will be too painful for me to see you again if I can't be yours. Head out to the west for that is where he rests," said the girl.

The young man was upset by this sudden change in his plan, but he was brave and had great love in his heart for the young woman. "I will venture to the ends of the earth in search of Sun and demand that he give me permission for you to be my wife."

"Have courage, my love," the girl said and then returned to her lodge.

Not knowing where to go or how to begin his journey, the young man sat down by the river and covered his head with his hands. After some sulking and self-pity, he got up and went to the home of an old woman who had been kind to him when he was a child.

"Could you please make me something to put on my feet? I have a long journey ahead of me," he said to the old woman. She agreed to help the young man in his quest and made him seven pairs of shoes. She also gave him a bag full of dried meat, berries and fat. The young man thanked the old woman and set off on his journey to find Sun.

Climbing a small hill, he looked back to the place where the beautiful girl waited for his return. A sudden chill went through his body when he thought of the possibility of never seeing her or his people again.

He did not know what kind of dangers awaited him on the path or if Sun was a kind or vengeful god. With a heavy heart, he gazed upon his village a final time before beginning his journey.

For days, he travelled through great expanses of prairies, crossed mighty rivers and climbed up and down majestic mountains. With each passing day, his sack of provisions got lighter and lighter. Walking along a path one day, Scarface stumbled upon the home of a coyote. "Excuse me, sir," he said. "I'm looking for the home of Sun. Do you know where I might find it?"

The coyote thought for a moment and then said, "I am a traveller like yourself. I have been all over these mountains, valleys and prairies, but I have never crossed paths with the home of Sun. However, I know of someone who might be of assistance in your quest."

"Please tell me," said the boy eagerly.

"Go to the home of the owl. He is most wise and sees the world from high in the sky. If anyone is to know the location of Sun, it should be him," said the coyote.

Scarface thanked the coyote and travelled for two days until he reached the home of the owl.

"You are not from around here," said the owl. "Why are you here all alone?"

"You must help me, dear brother," pleaded Scarface. "If I do not find Sun, I will not be able to marry the most beautiful woman in the world. Have pity on me!"

"You seek Sun?" said the owl. "Unfortunately, my brother, I do not know where he lives. I have flown over many expanses of land and water and I have never seen the home of Sun. However, there is someone who lives in that forest just over that ridge who might be able to help you. You will know him when you see him."

The young man went into the forest to find this person the owl spoke of, but he did not see or hear anyone. He sat down on a rock and cried out, "Please hear my calls! I need help. All my shoes are worn out and my provisions are almost gone. I will most surely die!"

It was silent for a moment and then a voice called out, "What is it?"

The young man looked about and spotted a large black bear, who suddenly appeared before him.

"The girl I want to marry gave herself to Sun. I'm trying to find his home so I might ask him for her."

"Ah," said the black bear. "I know exactly where he lives. Wait until morning as it is almost dark, then I will take you along a hidden trail that will lead you to him."

Early the next morning, the black bear led the man to the trail and pointed out the direction he had to take. Scarface walked for hours along the narrow trail until he arrived at a place where the land meets the great waters. He looked out across the vast expanse of water and could not believe his eyes.

He had seen big lakes and rivers, but never had the land suddenly disappeared in front of him like this. Looking out across the ocean, Scarface felt his heart sink. "If Sun's home is on the other side of this water, I'm surely going to fail and never see my beloved again," he said out loud to himself. "I shall remain by the water's edge and die."

Just as he was about to lose all hope, the water suddenly began to churn before his eyes and a giant turtle emerged.

"Why are you sitting on the shore and crying?" asked the turtle.

"I've come here to die. I have failed in my quest to reach the home of Sun and to win my love's heart. I have no food, and my clothes are falling apart at the seams. I can't return home, so I will just lay here until I return to the earth," said the boy mournfully.

"Today is not a good day to die," replied the turtle. "I'll carry you safely across the waters. There are many giants and monsters below the dark waves. Only with me will you reach your journey's end. Now climb on board."

Scarface jumped on the turtle's back, and they moved through the water with incredible speed.

Within moments, they reached the other side of the great ocean. Before getting off the turtle's back, the young man turned his head and looked back to where he had come from. He could not see the land from which he had started his journey.

"Listen, young traveller," said the turtle. "You are now within a few steps to the lodge of Sun. Follow this trail in front of you and you will reach your destination."

Scarface hopped off the turtle's back and started to walk up the trail. He had expected to find a land filled with wonderful and magical things, but instead, he only saw evidence of death and destruction. Lying in the grass and buried in the dirt were the shields and weapons of long-dead warriors.

Scarface walked among the artifacts of the dead and began to quake with fear. Then he saw the reason many of those warriors had come to these distant shores. All along the path lay the most ornate stones and golden feathers. "If these warriors perished before even getting to Sun's door, what chance do I have at succeeding?" he thought to himself. Trying not to make a sound, he stepped over the weapons and shields and continued on his journey.

Scarface was about to enter through a gateway formed by arching trees when a young man jumped out from behind a tree. He wore the most luxurious clothing Scarface had ever seen, his long golden hair flowed down the length of his back and his skin reflected the light in the most peculiar way.

The young man said to Scarface, "Stranger, were you going to steal the weapons along the trail?"

"No. I thought they must have belonged to someone else, and I knew I had no need for any such armaments," replied Scarface.

"What's your name?" asked the bright-looking man.

"My name is Scarface, and I come from a land far away."

"My name is Morning Star, and Sun is my father. Why have you come to this place?" he asked.

"I seek an audience with your father," said Scarface, trying to hide the fear in his voice.

"Very well then, follow me," said Morning Star as he led him to the front door of the house of Sun. "My father is not home right now, but he will return this evening. Don't be afraid. There's nothing to fear here. Now rest. You have journeyed far and no doubt must be tired."

Scarface walked into the house and before him stood Moon, Morning Star's mother and wife of Sun. She was a lovely woman, dressed in glowing white robes. She spoke to Scarface in the kindest of voices. "Why have you travelled so far from your people?" she asked.

"Most kind lady, I have come to speak with your husband. I have fallen in love with the most beautiful girl in all the lands, and I want to take her hand in marriage," he said passionately. "She gave herself to Sun and I have come to ask for her."

When it was time for Sun to return home, he entered his house and immediately set his eyes on Scarface. "I thought I smelled a person," said Sun.

"Father, it's okay. He's a good man," said Morning Star. "He saw all the riches we have and did not take anything. He has travelled far for a noble cause."

"Very well then," said Sun. "You're welcome to stay in our home for as long as you wish. Since you have already met with my son, you can be his friend."

The next day, Sun awoke Scarface and Morning Star, and after their morning meal, Sun called them outside. "Go with Morning Star to hunt," said Sun to Scarface. "But don't go near the ocean. It's the home of the great sea monster that has killed many of our children."

"Please heed my husband's advice," added Moon. "Morning Star is our only child left. Please watch over him."

After packing their gear, Scarface and Morning Star left the house and set out to hunt. For most of the day, they roamed the forests surrounding the house, but then they ventured closer to the water, where Morning Star caught sight of the giant sea monster.

"Come," said Morning Star. "Let's go and kill that beast. He has tormented my family long enough."

Before Scarface could say a word, Morning Star bounded down to the beach and jumped into a canoe. "Come on!" he yelled.

"We can't go there!" screamed Scarface. "The sea monster swims these waters and will surely kill us. Come back!"

Morning Star would not listen, so Scarface was forced to follow. He knew that if anything were to happen to Morning Star, Sun would hold him responsible. As they pushed off from the shore, something from underneath the dark waters bumped their boat. Scarface readied his weapons for the fight. He couldn't let anything go wrong or else he might never see his beloved again.

The waters began to churn, and beneath the boat arose the most gruesome of sea creatures. It had the huge body of a whale and the head of a serpent. Its eyes settled directly on Morning Star, but before it could strike, Scarface threw his spear and hit the beast in the neck, killing it instantly. He then tied a rope to the monster, and he and Morning Star hauled it to shore. Scarface drew his knife and cut off the monster's head.

When they returned to the home of Sun, Scarface showed the head to Moon and she began to weep with joy. When Sun returned home, he was over-joyed at the story of their encounter with the beast. "I cannot thank you enough for saving my only son from that horrible monster. I am indebted to you. What can I do to repay you?" Sun asked Scarface.

"I have gone on this long journey to ask you to release my beloved to me. She told me that she had given herself to you and that she could not marry another. It was she who sent me on this journey."

"I have watched over all of creation since time began," replied Sun. "I know you're a good man and that the girl has been faithful to me, so I will give her to you. I am the chief of everything, and what I say is the law. Everything was created by me—the earth, the mountains, the animals, the river and the people. I can never die, and although winter's cold weakens me, I always return fresh and full of energy in the spring. So it is my will to let you marry your beloved. Now come with me. I want to show you something."

Sun took Scarface's hand and Scarface was sud-denly blinded by a flash of light. When he opened his eyes, he found himself standing on the edge of the sky looking down upon all of creation.

"Listen, for I am going to tell you something that you must remember," said Sun to Scarface. "You will take this knowledge and pass it on to your people. When someone is sick, you must build a medicine lodge when the person recovers. You will build this lodge in the shape of the world—round and with walls. It's there that you will bring the sick to be healed. You must also build a sweat lodge made with 365 sticks. Paint the top half red—that is me—and the bottom half black, which is the night. Now come close to me."

Scarface cautiously approached Sun, who held out his hand and gave Scarface a medicinal powder. Scarface took the powder and rubbed it over the scar on his face, and it instantly disappeared.

"Now you are healed and ready to greet your new wife," said Sun. "Take these eagle feathers. They are to be worn by the new husband and wife who build the medicine lodge."

The next morning, as the young man prepared to return to his village, Morning Star and Moon gathered to say goodbye. Sun had already departed and was high in the sky. Moon and Morning Star gave the young man many beautiful gifts and new clothing for his triumphant return home.

"Do not take the long way home. Follow the white trail in the sky and it will lead you directly to your village," said Moon.

The young man followed the white trail, which is the Milky Way, and left the world of Sun to begin his journey back to his village.

When he got closer to his village, he looked down on it from a nearby hill and could see that the people were preparing for a community dance. Everyone, even the chief, was there.

Covering his face with the hood of his new cloak, the young man walked into the centre of the gathering and removed his cloak. The people could hardly believe their eyes. Before them stood Scarface, but he no longer had the mark on his face and was dressed in the finest of clothes. All the people rushed to his side and asked where he had received such nice garments and how he had come to lose his scar. The young man remained silent. Then the crowd parted, and the beautiful girl walked toward him. She looked at him and smiled.

"The trail was long and the journey was filled with danger, but I have returned," said the young man. "I have brought two eagle feathers from he who you swore yourself to. The feathers are the sign to you that you are now free to open yourself to another."

Soon after, the young couple were married and they built the first medicine and sweat lodge, as Sun had requested. Sun was happy. He rewarded the couple with a happy life and several children. After living a long life, one night the couple went to bed but did not wake. Their spirits had departed for another world.

How the Loon Got its Necklace

ONE DAY, AS OLD MAN SAT facing the bright rays of the early-morning sun, the sky slowly lit up with a brilliant array of colours broken only by the clouds. The light shone down on the forest, breaking through the leaves of the trees and hitting the ground in selected spots. The shimmering leaves of the aspens waved in the wind, looking like polished gold in the sun, and the spruce and pine trees stretched skyward, beyond his village.

Overhead an eagle floated effortlessly in the morning air, soaking up the sun just as Old Man was doing. Old Man could hear the creatures of the forest rustle about in the underbrush running for cover as the eagle cried out above. All this beauty Old Man could only feel and hear because not long ago the shadows of the night had clouded over his eyes. Old Man was sad.

While sitting outside in front of his lodge, he was shaken out of his calm by the nagging voice of his wife. "Why are you not out making arrows and other weapons like other men who live in the dark?" she whined. "You're no longer the same medicine man you once were. The people don't visit you anymore, and they openly mock your abilities to heal them."

"You don't know anything of what you speak," replied Old Man.

"I hear the people complain," said his wife. "They say all you can think of is to do things in four. You say things like, 'When the frog croaks fours times, seek out spruce sap for your cough.' Or, 'Place four birch leaves on the belly of your pregnant wife and she will have a son.' Your medicine is thought of as lies by the people."

"Four is my medicine sign. It was given to me in a dream when my totem and animal spirits were revealed to me," he said.

"Call upon your spirits now to come to our aid. We don't have much food and we do not have the respect of the village," she said.

"I will when the time comes."

Old Man was always sad. The only time he found relief from his dark life was when he heard the quivering laugh of the loon carried along by the winds. It was only then that a smile crossed his face and a slight joy entered his heart.

In time, the cool winds of autumn gave way to the cold embrace of winter. Hunting had been bad in the autumn, but when the snows arrived, the situation became desperate. The cold was especially harsh that year, and a constant fear of hunger gripped the hearts of Old Man and the people of his village. The best hunters in the village were sent out far into the wilds, but they came back with barely enough to feed their families, let alone a village. And the snows continued to fall.

One night while lying awake in his bed and shivering from the cold, Old Man heard the distant cry of the loon. The sound calmed him instantly, and he fell asleep. However, his sleep was not peaceful, and he had a dream.

The dream repeated itself four times that night, and each time it was the same. The dream began with a hungry pack of wolves descending on the village. Closer and closer the howling became until the howls turned into the screams of his people. As sudden as sleep had come to him, it left Old Man when the haunting call of the loon sounded in the distance.

When dawn finally arrived, Old Man stumbled to the chief's lodge and warned him about the pack of wolves from his dreams. "They will come in four days and will spare no one, not even a child," said Old Man.

The chief and his council held back their laughter, but Old Man knew what they thought of his warning. "We have heard enough of your warnings, Old Man. Go back to your wife. I have more pressing matters to deal with," said the chief.

Word quickly spread of Old Man's prophecy, and the villagers laughed at him mercilessly. They no longer believed in his powers as a medicine man. All he said in response to their taunts was, "When the time comes, you will all see."

As the sun descended on the fourth day and night enveloped the sky, an eerie calm swept through the village. No sounds could be heard except for the cold winter winds whistling through the bare branches of the trees. The silence was broken by the sound of the savage howling of the wolf pack. Terror spread through the village in a wave. They had made fun of Old Man before, but now they believed his words. People hid in their homes and cowered in fear.

Old Man sat in his house and waited. The howling suddenly stopped. Silence. Then he heard screams of terror and the ravenous sounds of wolves tearing flesh apart. The wolves tore at women and dragged little children away into the dark forest. It felt like hours before the warriors finally drove away the wolves with fire and weapons.

Each night, the wolves returned to the village, and each night more people were killed or went missing. A dark, all-consuming fear had taken hold of the people—even the bravest warriors were afraid.

The howling and killings continued for many nights until one day the chief called together a council and begged Old Man to honour them with his wisdom. This time they listened.

"Please tell us what we can do!" cried the chief.

"Despite your mockery for all these years, I can no longer stand by and watch as our people are devoured. I will go into my dreams and return with an answer for the village," said Old Man.

For several hours that day, Old Man slept while the villagers waited for his advice. He lay in his bed but could not lose himself to the dream. Then he heard the distant call of the loon and instantly passed into the dream world. In his dream, for the first time, he found that he could see clearly. It was the most spectacular sensation he had ever felt. Before him was a beautiful lake shimmering in the midday sun. It was summer and all the flowers and the trees were in full bloom.

"Have I passed into the world of the dead?" he thought to himself. Old Man peered across the lake, and out in the distance he could see a small black figure floating on the water's surface. He called out to the figure, and in the blink of an eye it was before him. It was his spirit animal, the loon.

Covered in black feathers, the loon looked at Old Man with its red eyes. Without a word, the loon placed exquisite bows at Old Man's feet and then took to the sky. As Old Man looked at the gift, he heard the loon's familiar song and in an instant was awake, back in his lodge.

Old Man held his eyes shut not wanting to believe he was still dreaming, but when he opened his eyes, the world was still swallowed in shadows. Everything was as it had always been, except in his hands he held a bow. Although he could not see it, Old Man knew he was holding something magical. After getting up, he also noticed that he no longer stumbled around. He was blind, but his feet carried him about the village with the confidence of the sighted. Old Man walked over to the lodge of the chief.

"I had a dream," said Old Man. "Bring me all your best hunting arrows and I will rid the village of the wolves."

"But you are blind. How will you shoot the wolves if you cannot see them?" asked the chief.

"Give me your best arrows and hide yourselves tonight. I will rid the forest of this pack of wolves."

That night began like the others before. As night pulled darkness across the sky, the wolf pack began to howl into the winds, breaking the silence in the air. Old Man walked to the centre of the village, held his bow up high and waited.

The howling stopped, replaced only by the sound of the wolves' feet hitting the cold snow-covered ground. The wolves burst through the cover of the forest, their heavy breath creating puffs of smoke in the cold night air. Old Man raised his bow, quickly loaded an arrow and pulled the string taut. The wolves stopped at the sight of Old Man.

One wolf began to charge Old Man, its mouth already open, teeth dripping with saliva. Old Man lifted his weapon and pulled the string back. The arrow whistled off the bow and streaked through the darkness, hitting the beast directly in the eye. With a heavy thud, the grey wolf hit the ground dead. Although Old Man could not see the wolves with his eyes, through the guidance of his spirit animal the loon, he knew where to aim his arrows.

Old Man's bow sang as his arrows glided through the air, each one finding its target with deadly accuracy. The cries of the dying wolves shattered the silence of the night, their great grey bodies pouring crimson pools of blood into the white snow. With most of the pack decimated by the hand of Old Man, the wolves that were still alive fled for the refuge of the forest. The hungry people of village then feasted on the flesh of the slain beasts. The remaining desperate wolves tried attacking the village several times, but with each attempt, Old Man and his powerful bow kept them at bay. In time, the snows finally melted, the wolves no longer came and the deer returned to the forests. The people were happy once again.

Early one summer morning, Old Man was sitting by his home soaking up the warm sun when he heard a faint cry off in the distance. It was the haunting song of the loon blending in the rush of the wind. Old Man was dressed in his finest clothes and around his neck was his most prized possession—a necklace made of brilliant white shells. Following the sound of the loon's call, he found himself standing on the shores of a lake.

Suddenly, he heard the call of the loon directly in front of him. Kneeling down, Old Man blindly reached out and touched the surface of the cold water. "Spirit guide," said Old Man. "Thank you for your guidance in my people's most darkest hour. I thank you for granting me the strength to defeat the beasts."

"Your hand defeated the wolves. I was there only to guide you," replied the loon in a soft musical voice.

"Now that my people have been granted safety, I have only one thing to ask of you," said Old Man.

"Ask me for anything," replied the loon.

Old Man took a deep breath. "For many years, I have stumbled about in darkness deeper than the night. Even in my dreams I have known only black. I beg of you to restore my eyes so that I may look upon a world that is probably more beautiful than I imagine it to be every day."

"You have believed all your life. When people doubted you and your faith in my guidance, they mocked you, but still you believed. For that, I will reward you," said the loon. "Jump on my back and I will grant your wish."

Old Man reached out, found the wing of the loon and then jumped on its back. Holding on firmly, the loon raced out to the middle of the lake and said, "Keep your eyes shut until you can no longer hold your breath."

The loon dove deep within the dark waters, and when Old Man could no longer hold his breath, he opened his eyes. The cold water stung his eyes and he felt intense pain. He immediately closed his eyelids, and the loon returned to the surface. Back on the shore of the lake, the loon said, "Now open your eyes slowly."

Old Man's heart began to race as his eyes opened onto a whole new world. It was as if he was looking at heaven itself. He was blinded by a great light, but it soon began to fade and the world unfolded before him. When he turned around, he clearly saw the great loon floating effortlessly on the water.

"Thank you, great and powerful spirit!" said Old Man. "How might I repay the gift you have given me?" He looked all about him for something he could give the loon, but then he thought of the perfect gift.

Removing the white shell necklace from around his neck, Old Man's trembling hands stretched out over the water and placed his most treasured possession around the loon's neck. The shells glided down the bird's black feathers and shone in the midday sun. Some of the shells fell from the necklace and landed along the loon's back and wings. The loon raised its head toward the sky and sung its haunting cry.

Old Man watched as the loon took to the skies, with its glistening feather necklace reflecting the light from the sun. Old Man returned to his village. He was finally happy.

Origin of the Narwhal Tusk

MANY GENERATIONS AGO, a woman lived with her young son and daughter in an isolated village. They were a close family and kept to themselves most of the time. The woman's son had been born blind, and the mother felt embarrassed. She always treated her son poorly and blamed him for her troubles. One day, tired of her life in the village, the woman gathered all her belongings and left with her children.

On their journey, they were caught in a snowstorm and were forced to build an igloo to wait out the bad weather. For days, they remained inside the igloo, but the storm continued to rage outside. Hunger began to eat away at their stomachs. If they were to venture outside, they would surely die in the storm, but they would starve if they stayed in the igloo any longer.

The small family decided to wait, hoping the storm would let up. Then one day, a large white bear came up to the ice window of the igloo and looked at the three people with his large eyes. The woman and her children could hear the giant beast's footsteps even above the noise of the storm as the animal circled the igloo. The bear appeared again at the window, one eye pressed up against the ice. No doubt it was looking for food.

"It's a white bear!" screamed the woman to her son. "You will shoot it for us. I will bend the bow and aim it for you, but you shall be the one to release the string."

The mother pulled back on the string with all her strength and aimed the bow at the window. The boy released the string. The arrow flew through the ice window, shattering it to pieces, and then they heard a heavy thud. Not long after, the storm stopped.

The mother said, "Oh no, you missed the bear! The arrow struck the wall and is stuck there. Your blindness has once again cursed us and we will starve."

The boy was blind, but he could see through his mother's lie. In fact, the arrow had struck the bear directly in the heart.

"The bear has been scared off by your missed shot," the mother said to her son. Then she whispered into her daughter's ear, "We will keep all the meat to ourselves. He has been dragging us down for too long. We will sneak outside, drag the bear away and eat the meat for ourselves."

The boy knew what his mother was up to but didn't say anything. He could smell the bear meat cooking, and he could hear his mother licking her lips in anticipation.

When the meat was ready, the mother and daughter fell into their food like a pack of hungry wolves. As the daughter ate, she allowed little bits of meat to roll down onto her clothes. She did this several times until her mother said, "You seem to be eating a lot. You've been gorging yourself on the meat, and yet you continue to eat like you are still hungry."

After eating her fill of the delicious bear meat, the mother eventually fell asleep. The young girl immediately woke her brother and fed him the bits of bear meat she had been saving for him. He was so thankful to his sister that he began to cry. He cried so much that he exhausted all the water in his body and suddenly felt thirsty.

"Can you lead me to some open water, sister? I am so thirsty," he said.

The young girl gladly took her brother outside and led him down a path to some water. When they arrived, the boy told his sister to return to the igloo. He did not want her to see how sad he had become. "Sister, lay out some stones along the path so that I might feel my way back to the igloo." She did as he requested, placing large stones all along the path.

The boy sat by the water's edge and drank until he was no longer thirsty. The sadness in his heart remained over his mother's deception. He began to weep again but was interrupted by the sound of a bird singing. A snowy owl had landed beside him. "Cry not, young one," said the owl. "Hang onto my neck and I will help you with your problems." The boy grabbed onto the owl's neck and together they soared high into the sky.

"We are going to dive through the clouds now. Every time we do, I want you to open your eyes," said the owl. The boy did as he was told, and each time the owl folded his wings and plunged through the white clouds, the boy forced open his useless eyes. At first he did not understand why he was asked to do this, but then something began to happen.

"How are you feeling?" asked the owl.

"This is incredible. I can see light! I'm beginning to see!" screamed the boy.

After the 10th dive through the clouds, the boy could see everything. He could see the owl he held onto, he could see the clouds below him and he could see the landscape beneath them.

"You are okay now, boy," said the owl. "Return to your family."

The boy thanked the owl and watched it fly off into the distance. The boy at once ran back to his mother's igloo. He could see that a bear skin had been stretched out to dry in the sun.

"Mother, I have returned, and now I can see!" exclaimed the boy. "Where did the bear skin come from?"

"It's the most wondrous of miracles that you can see!" she said. "That bear skin was left here as a gift by some stranger. What luck we had!"

The boy knew she was lying.

That day, the mother, the daughter and the son packed up their belongings and returned to their village. As it would take several days to get back to the village, they needed to hunt for food. On the way, they happened to walk by a break in the sea ice where they spotted several large white whales off shore.

The boy, now with his sight restored, prepared his harpoon for the hunt. To anchor the harpoon to the shore, he tied a line between his sister's legs and the weapon, according to tradition, so that the harpoon would not be lost and she would get an equal amount of meat when the hunt was over.

"Tie another harpoon line to me," said the boy's mother. This was done.

The boy then took the harpoon that was attached to his sister and threw it at one of the smaller whales. His sister held onto the whale while her brother took aim with the second harpoon.

"Quickly!" yelled his mother. "The other ones are getting away."

So the boy threw the harpoon at the biggest of the white whales and struck it directly in the back. The whale was wounded but had enough energy to swim farther out to sea. The mother tried to keep her balance and hold onto the whale, but the beast was too strong. The whale dragged her across the ice before pulling her into the frigid waters.

In a panic, the whale dove beneath the surface, taking the boy's mother down with him to the bottom of the icy sea. When they resurfaced a few minutes later, the mother gasped for air and tried to scream for help, but her words were muffled because the whale quickly dove under the water again. When they returned to the surface, the woman screamed to her son, "Please help me! Toss me the spear!"

The boy picked up his spear and threw it to his mother. The spear flew through the air and hit the woman directly in the nose. The spear lodged below her eyes, stuck in her skull. The boy's mother was dragged down into the deep waters, never to return.

There in the deep magical waters, the boy's mother was transformed into a narwhal. Her body was covered in blubber, and where her nose had been was the spear, which was now a long, twisted tusk. This is what happened long ago. This is how the narwhal got its tusk.

Why We Die

WHEN THE CREATOR MADE the first peoples out of the mud, he did not give them any instructions or tell them how to live. That job was given to Raven, but Raven was not one to do something right away if it did not suit him and therefore the first peoples on earth were left alone to learn how to survive in nature.

Among those first peoples to inhabit the earth, two women became pregnant. Raven had told the people that this might happen after intercourse, but as this was the first time it occurred, the people of the tribe had no idea how to treat these swelling women. For nine months, they called out to Raven for guidance, but he never came.

The people of the first tribe thought Raven would eventually come along, but then one day both women began to scream with pain. One woman was given a stick to hold onto while giving birth, and the other was given a stone. The child born to the woman who had held the rock died immediately after birth. The woman began to weep at the loss of her baby.

It was then that Raven suddenly appeared and spoke to the women. "I'm so sorry I didn't come when you called. I've come too late to help you. It is now written that all people on earth will die." If the child of the woman who held the rock had survived, people would have lived forever. People would have been like the rock and lived for all eternity.

Then woman who held the stick gave birth, and humanity, like all trees, had to eventually die. People are like the trees of the earth. Some will live like the giant redwoods—they will live to an old age and eventually decay and die. Other trees will grow only to a certain height and then die. Death must come for people of all ages, for we are like the trees of the forest, never to see eternity.

Guardian of the Dead

WHEN THE FIRST PEOPLES were created and placed on earth, they did not know of death or disease, but then the Creator decided that people should not live forever and must pass into the world of the dead. Since the world was new, the Creator had not given the dead a place to rest, so he created an island far away and made a powerful spirit named Old Woman to be the guardian of this realm. She was given great powers, and all who entered the realm of the dead were only allowed to leave if she gave her permission.

Before death came to the first people, the idea that all living things must pass to the spirit world was a phenomenon of nature that they witnessed every day. But nature was different from humankind. The people saw the leaves change colour and fall to the ground with the coming of winter, but in springtime, life again returned. The trees grew, the flowers blossomed and the warmth of the sun brought a vigour back to the earth.

However, for the people, when someone passed on into the realm of the dead, they did not return. This left a great hole in the hearts of many people, who longed to be rejoined with their loved ones and achieve immortality. They had hoped that when it came time for the trees to blossom, their loved ones too would return to the earth again.

Raven saw that the people were dying and going away to the land of the dead. This was the natural cycle of life, but the people left behind in the world of the living were left in terrible grief. Sorrow swept the lands and gripped their hearts. They could do nothing but grieve for their lost loved ones all day and night. The feelings of loss darkened the people's hearts, made their face shallow and skin pale. Life on earth had become a miserable place as the people sat around lamenting the loss of their loved ones.

Raven had also lost some of his children, but he knew that one day when the Creator was ready, the dead would return and reunite with their families. This comforted Raven, but not Eagle. He had lost his wife and was consumed by grief. Eagle was a god of great power like Raven, but he was impatient.

"Let us go to the land of the dead and bring back our loved ones to end this suffering. Look before you, Raven," said Eagle. "Look at how the people throw themselves onto the ground, tearing at their hair and faces. The world is coming apart, and we can stop this."

Raven agreed with Eagle, as he secretly longed to be reunited with his children, and the two set out together toward the land of the dead. After they travelled for many days to the west and over many great bodies of water, they came to the edge of all known lands.

A great fog was rolling in off the water, blocking out the early-morning sun and sending a chill through Eagle and Raven's bodies. Raven called out for someone to answer but received no reply. The fog began to roll in heavier and enveloped Raven and Eagle. Now they could not even see each other. For several hours, they stood on the edge of the great ocean and called out for someone to answer.

As the light of day began to fade, the fog slowly began retreating, revealing an island off in the distance that had not been there earlier. Eagle's powerful sight spotted several houses on the island with smoke billowing out of their chimneys. Raven called out again, but no one answered.

"We have come all this way for nothing," said Eagle, who was beginning to grow impatient.

"No, they are there," answered Raven. "They are just asleep. The dead sleep in the daytime and come out at night."

When the sun had completely disappeared, Raven called out across the waters to the island of the dead. He had said only a few words when four spirits came out of the houses, got into their canoes and started toward the shore. The boats glided above the surface of the water as if pushed by unseen hands.

When they reached the shore, one of the spirits stood up and spoke, "I am Old Woman. This is my realm. Because you, Raven and Eagle, are gods, I will allow you passage into the land of the dead. But know this—if you upset the balance of my world, there will be a punishment."

Raven and Eagle climbed into the canoe and journeyed across the ocean into the realm of the dead. They found many spirit people there, and all were dressed in the most beautiful of clothes. The spirits could neither see nor hear Raven and Eagle when the two visitors tried to talk to them.

And then Raven saw his children and began to weep, but his sobs went unnoticed. The same thing happened to Eagle when he saw his wife.

This angered Raven and Eagle. Raven tried yelling into his children's ears, but they heard nothing. Eagle became so angry and frustrated that he tried to push one of the spirits, but his hands passed through it like a rock through water without it even noticing.

Angry at being unable to communicate with the spirits, Eagle took out a large basket, placed it over his wife and the children of Raven and closed the lid. The spirits were lighter than a feather and easy to carry.

Raven and Eagle ran to the boat with the basket and rowed quickly back to the realm of the living, but as they were getting close to the shore, Raven noticed that the basket they had placed the spirits inside was getting heavier. Soon a great commotion came from the inside of the basket. The spirits were knocking about and screaming in pain. Raven put his ear to the basket and listened. "Eagle!" he shouted. "The people are beginning to come to life!"

The basket grew heavier as the spirits began to change to earthly flesh and blood. Raven suggested they let the people out to ease the burden, but Eagle insisted they remain inside the basket. The farther away they got from the island of the dead, the louder the complaints from the spirits became.

Finally Eagle said, "I think it's okay to let them out now. We are far away from the realm of the dead, and they will not be going back."

Raven agreed, and when he opened the basket, the people jumped out. They instantly resumed their spirit form and floated above the water to return to their home. It was then that the guardian of the dead appeared.

"I warned you not to meddle in my affairs!" yelled Old Woman. "For your interference in my realm, it is not you who will be punished but your people. The dead will never come back to life. If it had not been for your interference, the spirits would have returned every spring like the trees and flowers. But it's your folly that causes the people to never again see their loved ones until they join me in my world."

Since then, when people die, they never come back to life. They remain on the island of the dead for all eternity. The people were sad to hear that their loved ones would never return, but Raven told them that the spirits of their loved ones were now living in peace and happiness in the realm of the dead, and that when people die, they will join them. This comforted the people, and they were able to move on with their lives, knowing that one day they would see their loved ones again.

The Guardian Quest

WHEN I WAS A YOUNG BOY, my grandmother told me about the animal guardian spirits. She used to tell me about the most wondrous things. She told me that spirits were everywhere in nature and that if you looked, listened and were strong enough, you could hear them calling to you. After I heard these stories, my grandmother would often find me outside with my ear to a tree, listening for its spirit to come and speak to me.

She told me that the spirits make everything in the world work. Spirits make the grass and trees grow, and they cause the winds to blow and the clouds to float across the sky. Every animal and every bird is imbued with a powerful spirit. When I asked my grandmother if our people had spirits, she told me that when a boy is young, he must go out into nature on a guardian spirit quest. The guardian spirit is with you throughout your life and protects and guides you along the way.

She told me how the boy begins his spirit quest with a ritual cleansing using clear water and then ventures into the forests for four or five days without eating. By the fifth day, he should have a vision of his animal spirit guide. Only the physically and mentally strong can stay in the forest until the spirit comes to guide them. The animal spirit will often test the courage of the boy, and if he does not run away from the challenge, a voice will speak to him and give him the power of his spirit guide.

Upon returning from the spirit quest, the boy should not reveal what his vision has been. If he does, he will lose the power bestowed on him. It is only many years later, when he has fully matured, that he may reveal his spirit guardian to others. If the spirit is that of an Eagle, for example, the boy will wear an eagle feather as a symbol of his power and guardian.

When someone is sick, the boy may call upon his spirit guardian to make that person well. When he is in danger, the spirit can be called to help. If he goes to war, his spirit is the guide that gives him courage.

So important was the guardian quest that it defined your essence and gave you purpose on this earth. Without our spirit guides, we are just empty shells wandering the earth.

My favourite story that my grandmother used to tell me was of the boy on his spirit quest and how the first eagle came to this world.

The First Eagle

A FATHER WANTED HIS only son to secure the most powerful of guardian spirits when the boy reached the proper age for his guardian spirit quest. He wanted his son to have a vision that would grant him great powers and surpass all the other men of the tribe.

The boy knew how important this spirit quest was for his father, so he took extra care in preparing for his journey. He cleaned himself from head to toe—even under the fingernails—and did not speak to any of his friends for one week before the quest, lest they should distract him from his goals. While the boy cleansed himself and meditated in the sweat lodge, his father built him a small tent deep in the forest where he would wait for his vision. The father had planned that his son should fast longer than the strongest and bravest men of the village.

"My son, the time has come for your guardian quest," explained the father. "Take this clean mat with you out into the forest. Follow the path, and you will reach the tent I have build for you. You will sit there for 12 days, and at the end of your quest I will bring you food and water. Endure your fast like a true warrior and you will be rewarded with great power."

The boy obeyed his father's instructions and left the village. For several days, the boy lay quietly in the tent his father had made for him and waited for his vision to come. Every morning, his father went to the forest to check on his son, but the boy paid him no attention, laying motionless with no signs of discontent.

On the 10th day of fasting, the boy became increasingly agitated and broke his silence when his father came to check on him. "Father, in my dreams I see nothing but evil things. In my dream, I laid naked on the cold ground. I was not dead, but my body began to slowly decompose. I could feel the worms eating at my flesh, but I could not move. Please, Father, might I break my fast and continue this another day?" asked the boy.

"You cannot give up when you are so close to your goal," encouraged his father. "The spirits watch over you, and if you depart now, you will never attain a spirit guide. Wait a few more days and you will accomplish the incredible and be rewarded for your perseverance."

The son obeyed his father and continued on his spirit quest. Again the boy was besieged by bad dreams. The next morning when his father came to visit, the boy said, "Father, the nightmares are getting worse. This time I dreamt that I was falling from the sky, but there was no end."

"One more night and I will bring you your favourite meal. Hold on and you will be rewarded," said the father.

The boy dutifully obeyed his father's commands and lay motionless in the tent for another night.

The next morning, the father walked through the woods with a basket of food for his son. He was positive that all his son's effort would be rewarded with the most powerful of spirit visions. Instead, the father found his son in the most peculiar of manners. Looking through the opening in the tent, he found his son standing up completely naked and his body was painted a golden brown. His son was painting a yellow circle around his mouth. The father tried to get his son's attention, but the boy was lost in another world and kept screaming a song over and over:

"My father has destroyed my manhood,

My father has destroyed my future.

He would not listen.

He would not take heed

When his son was in most need.

It is freedom I seek.

I shall become a bird and take to the air.

My father will remain and suffer on land.

I will be free because he did not take heed

When his son was in most need."

The boy's father was in anguish and pleaded to his son, "Do not leave this earth! I need you! You're my only son."

The boy stopped chanting, slowly turned to his father and spoke in a voice that was not his own. "You will suffer on this earth. You forced your son to endure beyond his means to increase your own status among your people. I am his guardian spirit, and I shall give him another form so he can roam this earth free. We must go!"

The father tried to restrain his son, but it was too late. In a brilliant flash of light, the boy was transformed into the most beautiful, golden eagle.

He flew out of the tent and into the open sky. The father watched as his only son soared high above in the clouds, his great wings catching the winds and his keen eyes starring down on the world. Perching on a tree, he looked down at his father.

"I am Eagle. Please do not weep for me. I will be much happier now than I would have been had I remained a man. You will forever be able to look to the sky and see me. Your wish that I would be the most powerful among the tribe will go unanswered, but let them know I'll always be a friend to the people. Although I will win you no great battles, I'll always be a sign of peace and prosperity on earth. When my kind are in abundance, the world is healthy. This is where I'll bring glory to you. I'm free of the cares of the world, and I now hunt for my food in nature and sleep in the trees with my tribe. Go, Father, and return to the village to speak of my transformation and the arrival of the great golden eagle to this world."

Looking up to the sky, the golden eagle opened its beak and let out its distinct cry to the world for the first time and then soared up past the clouds.

The father returned to his village. He mourned the loss of his son every day, but if he wanted to feel close to him again, all he had to do was look to the sky.

How the Birch Became Scarred

OLD MAN WAS TRAVELLING across all the lands. One day, the air became so hot and humid that Old Man became tired. To cool down, he called upon the wind to blow across the land. The cool breeze made him feel better, and he continued calling it to blow harder and harder until there came such a fierce hurricane wind that Old Man was flung high up into the air.

Every tree he caught hold of while flying through the air became uprooted. Old Man was having a wonderful time in the cool air and grabbing onto trees until he caught hold of a birch tree. The tree didn't pull out of the ground.

When the wind died down and he had rested, Old Man began to yell at the birch tree. "Why do you have such strong roots that you cannot be pulled up like all other trees? I was having a good time in the cool wind until you spoiled my fun."

Old Man was so angry that he drew his sharpest blade and slashed the birch tree all over. This is the reason why the bark of the birch tree is marked up in such a manner.

Old Man Creates the Lynx

A LONG TIME AGO WHEN Old Man walked the earth, he came to a place where many ground squirrels were gathered around a fire playing a peculiar game. One of the squirrels allowed himself to be buried in the hot ashes of the fire until he began to squeal, at which time the other squirrels would pull him out. The winner of the game was the squirrel who could stay under the ashes the longest.

Old Man pretended that he wanted to learn the game and asked the squirrels if they could all show him how it was done. Since there were so many squirrels, Old Man suggested they all go into the ashes first—that way he could pull them out one at a time and finally decide a winner. The squirrels agreed, and Old Man covered all the ground squirrels with ashes except for one pregnant squirrel who was afraid for her unborn child's life.

When all the squirrels were under the ashes, Old Man warned the mother to run away so that there would be other squirrels left in the world. Old Man waited and waited until the squirrels under the ashes began to squeal, but he did not remove them. He left each squirrel in until they were well roasted. Old Man then ate so many of the tasty squirrels that he fell asleep by the fire. While he was asleep, Lynx came along and quietly ate the rest of the roasted squirrels.

Several hours later, Old Man woke up and saw that someone had eaten all his food. He followed the culprit's tracks until he came upon Lynx fast asleep after his big meal. Old Man was so angry that he grabbed Lynx by the ears, making them pointed, and shortened Lynx's head by smashing it against a stone. Old Man then pulled out Lynx's tail and stuck the end of it up the thief's bum, which turned the tip of his tail a dark colour.

Old Man then stretched out his legs and cast Lynx to the ground, saying, "You, Lynx, will always look like this, and you will be weak in the lungs so that you will never be able to run far. This is your punishment for stealing my dinner."

Why Raven Caws

LONG AGO, WHEN RAVEN still wandered the earth, he was flying along the coast when he came upon a village. He perched in a tree near the village and watched the people. The men had just returned from a fishing trip and the women were laying out the salmon on racks to dry. Raven waited and watched as the women finished hanging the fish.

When the women were finished their task and had walked away from the racks, Raven flew from the tree branch and swooped down to steal some of the salmon. He flew to a clear area in the forest to enjoy his feast, but while gobbling it down, a fish bone got stuck in his throat.

Blue Jay, who was sitting nearby, heard Raven struggling to breathe and jumped on his throat to get rid of the bone. But Blue Jay's efforts were unsuccessful and the fish bone remained in Raven's throat. And that is why Raven caws the way he does today; he is still trying to dislodge the bone from his throat.

Coyote and the Giant

WHEN THE FIRST PEOPLES walked the earth, the land was different from what you see today. The earth had many kinds of beasts and monsters that preyed on the people and made their lives miserable. Coyote was the only spirit that was kind to the people, although he liked to play tricks on them sometimes.

Coyote was wandering through the lands looking for tasty morsels to eat by the banks of a river. He had caught a salmon and was happily devouring it when a man came running up to him. His clothes were torn and dirty, and his body was covered in open sores. The man could barely talk because he was so exhausted. "Please...help...monster...people...dead...."

"What are you talking about? I've killed all the monsters of these lands. I'm the earth's greatest hero," boasted Coyote.

"No...swallowing monster!" cried the man weakly. "It consumes all."

Coyote was angry that a monster would dare to destroy his world. "Where is this beast now? I have killed titans before and shall defeat this beast now."

"To the north. There it swallows all. Even the people," replied the man before falling down and dying from exhaustion.

Coyote began his journey to find the beast. He travelled north following the river upstream. He came upon many lands that were once rich with life but now lay bare, destroyed by the swallowing monster.

All was lost. Not only had the monster swallowed the animals and the people, but it had also stripped the trees from the earth and the water from rivers.

Coyote walked past all the desolation and continued along the path until he eventually came to a high ridge. He could hear a great noise on the other side and feel the air being sucked from all around him. He knew he had reached the home of the monstrous beast.

Quietly, Coyote climbed the ridge to get a look at the beast. When he had reached the top, he peered over and could hardly believe his eyes. The first thing he noticed was the beast's incredibly large mouth—its width seemed to have no end. Perched on top of its massive head were six pairs of eyes and nostrils as big as mountains.

Coyote had never seen such a huge beast and watched as it snaked its way through the valley.

"If I am going to defeat this thing, I cannot use only my strength. I'll need to also use my cunning," he thought.

Coyote stepped out from behind the cover of the ridge and approached the beast. "You're the one swallowing everything. You seem great and powerful, but I'm sure I can swallow more than you can," challenged Coyote.

The beast stared down at Coyote and let out a deep earth-shaking laugh, its foul breath polluting the air. "Ha! Ha! You're a funny little one. How can such a small thing like you possibly challenge my greatness?" said the monster.

Coyote looked into the beast's mouth as it laughed and could see the tangled up lodges of the people's villages among the dirt and trees. "I think I can swallow you hole!" Coyote yelled at the beast. "Do you take my challenge?"

"I look forward to the easy meal," answered the monster. "You may swallow me first."

Although Coyote was small, he was truly powerful. Using all his strength, Coyote drew in his breath, which caused the air around him to move with the force of a hurricane. But the great beast did not move; it just sat there laughing.

"I now see that I am doomed," said Coyote to the beast. "Inhale me into the pit of your stomach so that I might not be alone on this earth since it would seem you have swallowed everything."

The monster took a deep breath and inhaled Coyote like a leaf in the wind. Coyote flew through the air, passed the wretched mouth of the beast and its rows of fangs and landed on its soft tongue.

Coyote looked around the wet, rotting mouth of the beast. He saw the bones of all the animals and people it had swallowed. It was the most awful sight Coyote had ever seen. He walked farther down the throat of the monster, where he came upon two young boys.

"What a miracle you are still alive!" cried out Coyote. "Do you know where the heart of this monster is located?"

The boys nodded their heads and motioned Coyote to follow them. Along the way, Coyote came across more survivors of the monster and told them to follow him to the heart.

"Gather up the bones of your loved ones. We will not rest for all of eternity in this awful place," said Coyote.

Now travelling deeper inside the body of the monster, Coyote and the others ran into several animals, and he told them to follow him as well. He met Bear, Beaver, Fox and Mouse, who had not been able to escape the powerful monster's grasp and were trapped inside the beast.

Coyote gathered up the wood he found along the way, and when he finally reached the chamber of the monster's heart, he lit a big fire. Smoke began to pour out of the beast's eyes, nose, mouth and anus.

"Once I have cut out the beast's heart, I want you all to escape through these holes. Follow the smoke and everything will be okay. Make sure you are out before the monster takes its last breath," instructed Coyote.

Coyote took out one of his knives and began to slice away at the muscles and veins holding the heart in place. With each cut, the swallowing monster let out a tremendous roar.

"All right!" Coyote told the people and the animals. "Get yourselves to the exits! Remember to kick all the bones out before you leave."

Coyote kept cutting away until finally the beast's black heart hung by a thin strand of muscle. He placed his knife to the muscle and in one swift motion detached the beast's heart from its body. In the throws of death, the monster's holes opened up and the people and the animals escaped. Coyote escaped too.

The monster fell dead and his openings began to close up. Coyote looked around him to make sure that everyone had escaped, but he could not find Beaver.

Suddenly Coyote heard a great stirring around the anus of the beast. He ran over to see what was going on and found the head of Beaver being pushed out of the tight opening.

Coyote grabbed onto Beaver's head and pulled as hard as he could. He managed to get Beaver out, except for his tail, which was trapped inside the monster.

Bear, who was the strongest of all the animals, grabbed onto Beaver and pulled with all his might, finally freeing Beaver's tail from the monster. But Beaver's once fat tail had flattened out and was stripped of his lovely fur. This is why the beaver's tail is flat and hairless to this day.

After making sure everybody was out safe, Coyote gathered up all the bones into separate piles.

He then cut into the monster and poured some of the beast's blood over the bones. Flesh instantly returned to the bones, and the people and animals again walked the earth.

After enjoying a great celebration and feast, Coyote left the people and returned to his life of solitude while the people and the animals began to rebuild their lives.

Coyote Versus Thunder

THIS WAS THE TIME WHEN the world was young, the time before the Great Flood, when there was great magic in all the lands and when people and spirits lived together in peace. Some spirits were poisoned by evil. One of these spirits was Thunder. He lived high in the mountains, way above the clouds.

For many years, Thunder tormented the people with his terrible rumblings. There was no escaping his wrath. From his perch on high, his gaze could penetrate the darkest corners of the earth.

When evil gripped at Thunder's heart, he would shoot flashing fire from his hands. This caused fires, and if the sparks struck people, they would burn instantly, turning them into a pile of ashes.

Many people died and many lands were left barren because of the wrath of the god Thunder.

The people were in a permanent state of fear. This was no life for them. The tyrant god used his power to shake the world. No crops could be grown, the men could not go out and hunt food for their families and couples were even too afraid to get close to one another to make children.

It happened one day that Coyote passed through one of Thunder's favourite villages to torment, and he saw that the people lived in misery. Coyote walked through what he remembered as one of the liveliest of villages, but he could not find a single person outside. It was as if all the villagers had disappeared or were killed. All about him were signs of destruction. The fields of corn lay burnt, animal bones lay scattered about blackened by fire and many of the lodges lay in piles on the ground. "What misery has befallen these poor souls?" he thought to himself.

Coyote was about to leave the village when he heard a noise coming from one of the lodges still standing. He pulled back the deerskin flap and found an old man sitting in the dark.

"Old man, why are you sitting in the dark? What happened here?" asked Coyote.

No answer came back. Coyote pulled back the deer skin flap further to let in some light. The old man was in a ragged state. His clothes were dirty and torn. It looked like he had not eaten for some time as his skin hung from his bones like the sagging branches of a willow.

"What has happened here?" Coyote asked again but got no response. The old man pointed to his ears.

"You are deaf?" asked Coyote.

Coyote grabbed the man's arm and tried to lead him outside, but he pulled away, falling back to the floor and cowering in the fetal position. Coyote left the man to his fears. Aroused by the noise of the old man and Coyote, several villagers emerged from their hiding places looking just as tired and dishevelled.

"Can someone please tell me what has happened here?" asked Coyote.

The people then told Coyote of the constant fear they lived in because of Thunder's wrath. They had not eaten in days because the hunters were afraid to go outside, and all the crops had been destroyed. Coyote had never known Thunder to act in such a manner, so he promised the people that he would take care of their problems. Normally, the people would have rejoiced at such good tidings, but without food, they had neither the energy nor the will to celebrate.

Coyote looked up to the sky and could see dark clouds forming. He did not know how he was going to get Thunder under control, but he knew he had to do something. If the situation continued in such a manner, Coyote would be without food and would have no fun.

Coyote left the village and began walking along the path that led to the highest mountains in the lands. It was the place where Thunder resided when he was not out terrorizing the people, and it was where Coyote would make Thunder calm his fury. For days, Coyote walked until he reached the base of the mountains. He transformed himself into a feather and was carried up by the winds.

From his perch in the mountains, Thunder looked down over the lands and noticed a strange feather floating in the air. "That looks like a feather, but it also appears to be an animal and a man," thought Thunder. "Just to make sure, I will send forth a torrential rain and mighty winds to knock it from the sky."

He reached out and pulled in the darkest of clouds from beyond the mountains, issued a hurricane force wind and created so much rain that the land below was nearly flooded, but still the feather floated in the air.

Angered by Thunder's hostile display, Coyote floated higher up into the mountains. Using his own powerful magic, Coyote called forth a violent storm of his own, sending flashes of light and rain down on Thunder's head. This angered Thunder greatly. "I thought I was the only Thunder god in the world!" he screamed. "How can a little feather have so much power?"

Coyote, in the form of a feather, floated up to the highest point in the mountains, then transformed back into his original form.

"I am Coyote, and I have great powers like yourself. You have terrorized the people and these lands for too long. I have come to stop you," said Coyote.

Jealousy began to flow through the spirit of Thunder at this theft of his power and dignity. In a furious rage, he sent down a deluge of water and flashing fire down at Coyote, but the wise old spirit dodged Thunder's attacks and answered back with a flurry of his own. Coyote's anger had never been so great. Flashing fire bolts shot out of his eyes and his thunder shook the earth itself. Coyote caused such a storm that even Thunder became worried.

However, Thunder was a vengeful god and would not be outdone by some puny, four-legged animal. With all his power, he issued a storm like the earth had never seen before. Rains poured down, flooding the lands below, flashes of lightning shot brighter that the sun and thunder rumbled so loud that it caused the grounds to shift. But Coyote did not dodge or blink. He created fire and noise more powerful than those of the god. It became a contest of power.

Thunder shot lightning down upon Coyote, tearing up the earth around him. Coyote answered back with lightning that sent shockwaves through the clouds and into the heart of the god. The enraged combatants rose up high into the sky and waged a fierce battle. The storm clouds blackened the sky and all the people below ran for whatever cover they could find.

Coyote and Thunder finally came together in the sky in the midst of the rain and clouds. Coyote pulled the god from his perch and they plummeted toward the earth, emitting bolts of fire as they fell. Like stars shooting through the sky, they fell to the earth in a bright flash of light. They hit the ground with such force that they shook the whole world. Coyote jumped on top of Thunder and began to beat him mercilessly with his fists. Finally the fallen god pleaded with Coyote for mercy.

"You do not deserve mercy!" yelled Coyote. "Heed my warnings, god. You shall no longer make it your business to terrify and rule over the people. They are free and shall be ruled by no one, not even the Creator. From this day forward, you may issue thunder and lightning but only on hot and humid days. If you destroy or kill any creature, I will return and break you."

Thunder heeded Coyote's warning and returned to his place in the mountains. Coyote had taken away most of Thunder's powers, and though he sometimes scares the people, he never kills.

Coyote wandered the lands for many years and along the way he fought several battles. He destroyed giants, pushed back floods and brought food to the people.

It is because of Coyote's kindness and courage that the earth became peaceful and a place where the first peoples could grow and have families. Without Coyote, the world would have remained in chaos, and the Creator would have wiped it all away as he had done before.

Giant Skunk's Offspring

LONG AGO, IN THE TIME before the world was remade through flood and fire, there existed Anniwaya, the giant skunk. Anniwaya was once a gentle and noble spirit, but evil corrupted him and turned his spirit and his insides rotten. His claws were as long as spears and just as sharp, his eyes were as black as night, he had teeth longer than the tusks of a walrus and his most foul weapon was the incredible stink that came out of his rear-end.

Everywhere he travelled, people knew Anniwaya was coming by the disgusting odour that overwhelmed the air. The people tried to hide from the stinking beast but finding them was Anniwaya's favourite pastime. If the people hid in the ground, he dug at the dirt with his claws to find them.

If they hid in caves, he waited until they finally emerged, spraying them with his revolting liquid, which would kill them instantly. The people called Anniwaya's spray, "the sickness." In that time long ago, it was the only sickness the people worried about.

Anniwaya was so good at rooting out the first peoples that after a while he was running out of people to find. He went to the north and could not find them. He travelled to the east and found only barren lands. He travelled to the west and found nothing but forest and a great water. Slowly but steadily, Anniwaya made his way south.

Far away from Anniwaya yet directly in his path, there was a camp of people. Several men were preparing for the hunt when an elder approached them with a warning. "Be careful and watch out for Anniwaya. I think I might smell something in the air," said the elder.

Despite the danger, the hunters needed to feed the people of the village and so they set out. After a few days, the group of hunters noticed a stench in the air and discovered a set of Anniwaya's tracks on the ground. "They look like empty ponds,' said one of the hunters.

"No, I have seen these before. It is Anniwaya," said the eldest hunter. "Let's go in every direction so that we can lead him away from the village.

Maybe some of us will escape and maybe some will die. We will all meet at the lake where the Giant Fisher lives. They are enemies, and if they battle, only one will come away alive."

The people knew Giant Fisher lived in the lake and they also knew he was not a harmful spirit like Anniwaya. So the hunters split up and went in every direction. The eldest hunter had not gone far when he came across an old woman sitting on a fallen tree. She had a bandage over her eyes and supported herself with a cane.

"What are you doing out here, old woman? Don't you know Anniwaya is coming?" said the hunter.

"I am blind and old. I don't move for anything," replied the old woman.

Just then, a great stench smacked into the nostrils of the hunter. Anniwaya had been following him. "If you will not cooperate, I must leave you behind," the hunter said to the woman.

"I will sit here," replied the old woman.

The eldest hunter ran through the forest and hid behind a tree. He watched as the giant skunk broke through the trees and stood before the withered old woman.

"Are you not afraid, old woman?" boomed the voice of Anniwaya.

"I am old and blind. Do your worst, skunk!" yelled the defiant old woman.

"Where are your people?" asked Anniwaya.

"They have all gone down to the lake. You should go and see them," said the old woman with a chuckle.

"Before I go, I will do you a favour. I will cure your blindness," said Anniwaya. He then turned around, raised his tail and sprayed the old woman with his foul odour. Psssatttt! The old woman disappeared.

Anniwaya put his snout to the ground and picked up the scent of the hunter. The eldest hunter, who had watched the old woman die, ran through the forest until he met up with the other hunters at the lake. They quickly hid themselves among the trees surrounding the lakeshore and waited for Anniwaya to arrive. They could tell he was close by because the stench in the air made it difficult for them to breath and the ground began to shake with each step the giant took.

The hunters called out across the lake, "Giant Fisher, Anniwaya is on his way and he wants to kill us! Can you help us?"

Far out in the lake, the water suddenly swelled and a long dark figure just below the surface began swimming toward the shore where the hunters stood. Fisher emerged from the water and towered over the hunters. Fisher might have appeared tall to the people, but his body remained low to the ground. He did not look like a mean animal, but Fisher was known for having one of the strongest jaws in all the animal kingdom—not even bear or wolf would cross paths with Fisher lest they get a chunk of flesh taken off them.

"I heard your call and I know what to do. That foul beast brings his stench into my lands and kills all the animals and people. I can deal with Anniwaya, but I will need your help," said Fisher. "You must remain brave. Stay out in the open. I will be hiding behind you in the cover of the forest. When Anniwaya turns to spray you, flee. I will do the rest."

The moment Fisher found his hiding spot, Anniwaya burst through the forest. The hunters wanted to run. The fear they felt and the overpowering stench of the beast were almost too much to bear, but they had promised Fisher they would be brave and stand their ground.

"You have avoided me long enough," said Anniwaya to the men.

"We do not fear you anymore, disgusting creature. Your spirit is weak and corrupt, and ours is strong!" yelled the eldest hunter.

This outburst made Anniwaya angry. He began breathing heavily and saliva flew from his mouth. He then turned around. The hunters fled for the safety of the forest. Just as Anniwaya lifted his tail to spray the men, Fisher rushed forward and pinched Anniwaya's hole closed with his jaw. The poison liquid could not escape. Anniwaya began to scream and jump around, but Fisher's jaw remained clamped. He stayed clenched onto Anniwaya until the giant skunk died. Anniwaya's own deadly liquid had poisoned him.

Fisher then said to the hunters, "Build me a large fire."

The hunters did as they were told. Fisher picked up the dead body of Anniwaya and tossed him into the flames. The skunk's ashes floated up high into the sky, and when they landed, each flake became a small skunk. The winds were strong that day and carried the ashes far, which is why we find skunks in so many different lands today.

How Muskrat Lost His Fur

Long, long ago in the time before the first peoples inhabited the earth, there lived the animal people. They looked like the animals we know of today, but they also walked about as humans do and lived as humans do. They lived together in peace, with only minor problems arising between the animal clans from time to time.

Among the animal people was Muskrat, who had the most beautiful tail in all the lands. It was covered in a luxurious coat of thick brown fur, and every day he lovingly combed it out. He loved to strut about the village showing off his tail, and everyone who came to his house had to listen to him talk about his tail at length.

Some of the villagers paid him no attention, but others were bothered by Muskrat's obsession with his tail. Others, more specifically Coyote, hated Muskrat's tail. Coyote was simply jealous because his tail was short, ragged and filled with nettles and dirt. Everyone in the village laughed at Coyote's sorry-looking protuberance, which filled him with even more rage and hatred for Muskrat's tail.

One day, the animal people decided to gather a council and have a big dance. As Coyote was swift on his feet, he was instructed to spread the news of the dance to the rest of the village. He passed by the houses of Badger, Bear and Lynx and gladly told them of the upcoming dance. Coyote invited everyone in the village, saving Muskrat for last. Coyote had to force himself, but he eventually passed by Muskrat's house to tell him of the dance.

"Oh, that sounds delightful!" said Muskrat. "But I will only grace the dance with my presence if I have a special seat brought out for me—one where everybody can see my tail. Only if this is done will I attend the dance."

"Make sure you come," replied Coyote. "I'll personally ensure that you have a special place to sit so that all the people in the village can marvel at your tail. And just for you, I will even send over Mouse to brush your tail before the dance so that you look your best."

Muskrat was pleased with this offer and thanked Coyote for his kindness.

Leaving Muskrat's house, Coyote immediately went to the house of Mouse and invited himself inside where they could have a long talk in private. Mouse was known in the village as the best hair groomer in all the lands.

The next day Mouse went to Muskrat's home. He said he had spoken with Coyote and that he was instructed to give his tail the best possible treatment.

"Please stretch out your tail so that I can begin," ordered Mouse. "I want you to close your eyes while I work my magic. I want it to be a surprise. When I'm done, your tail will look better than ever."

Mouse went to work on Muskrat's tail, and when he was finished, he wrapped the tail in strips of deer hide. "Now Muskrat," instructed Mouse, "make sure to keep your tail covered until the dance when you are ready to show everyone. I guarantee you will be the centre of attention."

On the night of the dance, everyone gathered at the dance hall. Muskrat strutted past the villagers and found the seat that Coyote had chosen for him. From his throne, Muskrat watched as the others danced. He stroked his tail lovingly and was getting more excited about revealing his new look to the crowd. Finally, when it was his turn to dance, he removed the cover from his tail and took to the dance floor.

The drummers began pounding on their instruments, and Muskrat swung his tail about while singing, "See my beautiful tail! My beautiful tail!"

While Muskrat danced around on the floor, all the people of the village turned to look at him. They began pointing and staring at him. "See how fine my fur is!" yelled Muskrat. "Take it all in, for not everyone is lucky to gaze upon such beauty."

But instead of the people applauding his tail like Muskrat had expected, they began laughing and saying cruel things.

"Look how the lizard's tail sweeps the floor!" someone shouted.

Muskrat stopped dancing and looked around as if someone was playing a joke on him. "How could they be laughing at me?" he thought. Then he looked down at his tail. All the fur from his tail was strewn about on the dance floor, and lying there in plain sight was his bare, brownish tail for all to see.

Coyote watched with delight as Muskrat for the first time in his life tried to hide his tail.

Muskrat did not know what to do, so he ran down to the river's edge and built himself a home made of mud and sticks in which to hide from the village. This is why Muskrat builds his home under mud and sticks—he is ashamed of his ugly tail.

The Creation of Everything

WE KNOW THERE WAS THE chief of the sky kingdom. He, who is also called the Creator, was in the sky kingdom before anything down on earth existed. He lived with his two grandmothers and together they watched over the earth from on high.

But there had been a world before this one. That world lasted a long time, and many beings lived here before the world today came into existence. They were the animal people, and they lived in a world created and shaped by magic.

In one village, the people began to hear rumours of a man in the south who was a skilled hunter. His name was Swift Fox, and he had killed so many game without much effort that everybody wondered how he was able to accomplish this. He had a weapon that the Creator had given him, but no one knew what it was.

Someone in the village said, "I wonder if we could get him to come to us if we sent for him?"

"That is a most excellent idea," said the village chief, White Crane. "We shall ask him to come to us. We'll tell him we're going to have a great dance in his honour. Tomorrow we will send someone down South to invite him."

The next morning, Crane sent a messenger to invite Swift Fox; he sent Green Snake, who was known to be a quick traveller. Although the home of Swift Fox was far, Green Snake arrived in one day. He gave the invitation to Swift Fox and told him about his people and the village. Swift Fox kindly accepted the invitation and told Green Snake he would leave in the morning.

Green Snake arrived back in the village the next day and told the people that Swift Fox was coming and that he would arrive in a day or two. While they waited for his arrival, the people cleaned up the village and prepared for the dance, which would be followed by a large feast after Swift Fox showed them how he was able to hunt so successfully.

Swift Fox left his lodge the next morning, and after some time, he came to a hill that overlooked the village of the people who had invited him.

Sitting down at the top of the hill, Swift Fox stayed there for a while and watched as the people danced and prepared for his arrival. After a few more minutes, Swift Fox descended the hill and entered the village.

Crane was the first to see the invited guest and greeted him. "Ah, noble Swift Fox, come sit by me!" he said to Swift Fox.

The people stopped dancing once they noticed Swift Fox had arrived and gathered around their guest. Crane had food brought out for their guest, and while Swift Fox ate, Crane said, "My grandfather's father and my people have all lived here for a long time. We have known many a great hunter, but never in our tales have we mentioned anyone that is as good as we hear you are. My people want to dance and sing. So tonight we shall celebrate your arrival and tomorrow we will go hunting. I am glad you have come, Swift Fox."

When Crane finished speaking, the people clapped their hands and started to dance in celebration of their guest. In the morning after they ate, a group of men gathered in the centre of the village. White Crane pulled his son Blue Jay aside and said, "When Swift Fox shoots a deer, make sure you run up to it quickly and remove the weapon. Hide it and say it disappeared. Return to me once you have succeeded."

So Swift Fox, Blue Jay and some others from the village all went out on the hunt. When they got to the base of a nearby mountain, they saw 10 deer off in the distance. Swift Fox shot without delay. Blue Jay ran as fast as he could to get to the deer first, but when he reached the animal, he found that Swift Fox was already standing over it and had taken out the weapon.

Swift Fox killed one deer after another until all 10 were hunted. Blue Jay returned home carrying one deer over his shoulder, but without the secret weapon of Swift Fox.

White Crane spoke to his son. "Where is the weapon? Did you see what Swift Fox uses to hunt?"

"No, Father," replied Blue Jay. "I don't believe there's a man in our village who can run as fast as Swift Fox; he is spectacular. I don't know what he uses to kill game, and I don't think we can wrench it from his hands."

That night, Red Fox went to visit Chief White Crane and said, "I'll go with Swift Fox tomorrow and see what I can do. We must do what we can to get his weapon from him because I don't think he will ever visit us again."

The next day, Swift Fox was thanking his hosts and preparing to return home, but White Crane used his power of persuasion to make him stay for one more hunt. The following morning after they woke up, the hunters ate their fill and left the village to hunt. Red Fox followed Swift Fox very closely.

They again saw 10 deer on the mountain. While Swift Fox stood up to shoot, Red Fox cheated by running ahead. The moment the weapon was shot, Red Fox ran with all his strength to the killed deer. He removed the weapon from the deer and hid it in his ear.

Seconds later, Swift Fox arrived. "You have stolen my flint!" he cried. "Give it back!"

"I didn't steal it. I have nothing of yours," said Red Fox, acting insulted. "I'm no thief. I have just arrived here like yourself."

"You have it," said Swift Fox. "I saw you take it."

"I took nothing. I only put my hand on the deer's head to thank it for its sacrifice," said Red Fox.

Swift Fox kept asking all day for his flint, but Red Fox would neither give it back nor admit that he had it.

As the sun went down and they returned to the village, Swift Fox said to Red Fox, "I saw you take my flint. It would be better for you to give it back to me. Better for you and better for your people. If you want to keep it, then keep it. If you do, though, you and your people will pay for this. There will be much suffering over this injustice."

Swift Fox then left the village and travelled back to his home.

White Crane gathered his people in the sweat lodge. Red Fox pulled the flint from his ear and held it in his hand for all to see. It was just a tiny thing.

"When I took this, Swift Fox became angry and departed for his home with the most dire of warnings," said Red Fox.

Badger was the first to speak. "You have done wrong. Swift Fox is strong and quick; you will see what he will do. He has great power—more power than you can imagine, and he will have his vengeance. He'll make us suffer terribly. He's stronger than we are. We will see something dreadful come soon."

"Quiet with you, Badger!" yelled White Crane. "Come and we shall see what we can do with such a small but formidable weapon."

The people of the village gathered around and discussed what they could do with the weapon. Some of the villagers had grown fearful after the warning by Badger and wanted to get rid of it, while some wanted to use the weapon for hunting.

"We must get rid of the weapon!" someone cried. "The village is in danger."

"Nonsense. Think of the food we might secure for the village if every hunt is successful," argued another. "And if anyone were to return to seek vengeance on us, we could use the weapon to slay them."

Chief White Crane then stood and declared, "I cannot risk the safety of the village for such a magical weapon. Who here knows what to do with this?"

Old Man Owl stood and spoke. "Give this to me and leave me in peace." Red Fox handed the flint to Owl. Once the Old Man was alone, he rubbed the flint in his hands and rolled it between his legs. As he worked, the flint it began to expand, and by the end of the night he had created a block four feet long and just as wide. Owl brought out the flint in the morning and showed Chief White Crane what he had done.

"See, now it is in disguise. Take it away from the village so that it might not curse us anymore," said Old Man Owl.

"Who among us will take this burden northward?" asked White Crane. "You, Grey Squirrel, will you take this block northward?"

"I'm too small. I most certainly will be flattened by its weight," replied Grey Squirrel.

"I'll take it," said Wolf. "I will carry it to the top of the mountain ranges in the north. Once there, I will shout and show you where I have put the block."

"Thank you. You will be rewarded for saving your people," said White Crane.

But Badger was not convinced. "You shouldn't have played with the flint," he said. "You should have taken it back to Swift Fox. Your plan will fail, and he will rain vengeance down on us."

Meanwhile, Swift Fox had returned home, and he called for his cousins Shooting Star and North Wind and told them about what had happened in the village to the north. His cousins were furious and wanted to seek revenge on his behalf. Together, they formed a plan.

Just before sunrise the next day, Swift Fox told Shooting Star to gather dry wood from the forest, while North Wind cleaned up a spot in front of the house with his mighty breath. Together they piled up the dry wood in the middle of the area. They waited a few moments, and when the sun rose beyond the edge of the earth, the wood burst into a great flame.

Shooting Star grabbed a piece of the fire and ran off to the east while North Wind took the fire and ran to the west. When Shooting Star reached the east where the sky meets the earth, he began to run across the dome of the sky, holding the flame up high and setting fire to everything he came across.

When North Wind reached the edge where the earth meets the sky in the west, he did the same. As Shooting Star and North Wind ran swiftly across the sky, they left a line of flame behind them that moved like an ocean wave.

Back in the village, Chief White Crane awoke that morning and organized a dance in celebration of ridding the village of the flint. The people were happy and relieved. Suddenly someone began to shout, "Look at the sky! It has been set on fire on both sides."

"This is the work of Swift Fox," warned Badger.

The fire sped across the sky, heading directly for the village. It was still far away, but the people could feel its flames licking at their skin. Clouds of smoke billowed behind the bright orange line of flames sending out a terrible roar as it burned everything in its path. The people of White Crane's village began to panic.

"My people, escape to the north!" yelled Chief White Crane. "We will meet with Wolf and the flint."

The people struggled to get to the mountains in the north, but they could not escape the heat. Looking behind them, they saw that their village had been engulfed in flames. The people were tired and weary. In the panicked rush north, Old Man Owl fell down, breaking his wing. Someone tried to help him to his feet, but he refused. "Leave me here. This is my fault for playing with the flint," he said. The people moved on, leaving Old Man Owl to be consumed by flame.

Chief White Crane rushed north to the top of the highest mountain, where he met Wolf.

Together, they lifted the flint block into the air and called out to the sky, "Take it back, but please spare us. Take it back!"

Swift Fox heard their cries on the winds but did nothing to stop his cousins from burning the sky. The fire moved across the earth, burning everything in its path. White Crane could go no farther. The chief and his people went up in flames and smoke toward the sky.

When Shooting Star and North Wind had carried the fire around the world and met in the north, they struck their torches together and threw them to the ground. Everything on earth had burned—the dirt, rocks, everything, except Mole and Green Snake, who hid deep under the ground. They barely escaped with their lives.

From his seat high up in the sky, the Creator of all things looked down onto the burning world. All he could see of his creation was waves of flame and smoke filling the air. Great plumes of smoke carried sparks high into the air where they stuck and became the stars. They have remained ever since that time when the first world burned.

"What am I to do about the fires?" the Chief of the Sky asked his grandmother.

"Go to the north part of your sky kingdom and seek out Old Man Winter Wind. He will be able to assist you in putting out the flames. Tell him what to do and he will do it. Make him bring his wife, Cloud. "

The Chief of the Sky called his most loyal and speedy servant, Hummingbird, to fetch Old Man Winter from his hiding place. "Hummingbird, go and find Old Man Winter and his wife. Bring them to me while I prepare to extinguish the earth."

Hummingbird left at once, and in a flash he had reached the home of the old man. "You must come with me," he said to Old Man Winter Wind. "The chief and creator of all things is in need of your help. The earth burns, and only with you and your wife's help shall we be able to put it out."

Old Man Winter grumbled and moaned, "Why should we help? Leave us alone!"

"You must come at once," said Hummingbird, buzzing around the ear of the Old Man. He had to ask several more times but eventually Old Man Winter gave in.

"Fine! I will depart at once. Come, Cloud, we are needed," he said to his wife.

Arriving at the lodge of the chief of the sky kingdom, Old Man Winter and Cloud paid their respects and set to work immediately.

Cloud punctured a hole in her side and water poured down upon the earth. Old Man Winter then took a deep breath and blew his cold wind, pushing the water to all corners of the earth. All the fires across the globe were put out, but Old Man Winter and Cloud did not stop once the fires were out.

Soon the waters began to rise up over the mountains, before flooding the hole in the sky. Now both worlds, the earth and the sky kingdom, were under water. The chief climbed to the highest mountain in his kingdom and yelled down at Old Man Winter and his wife.

"Please, that's enough! We have had enough wind and water. If you don't stop, I will be forced to stop you!" he screamed.

Old Man Winter calmed his fury, and Cloud ceased raining down, and together they returned to their home. When they left, all the water disappeared, leaving everything calm, dry and clear again.

The chief looked down on earth but saw nothing—no trees, no dirt, no life at all, nothing but naked rock, washed clean. He searched across the earth for life and found nothing except for a small piece of land that had collected some water and mud. Around that water was Mole and Green Snake.

The chief of the sky kingdom spoke to them: "You have survived many hardships. Take this water and mud, and spread it across the earth. Go and make mountains and valleys."

Mole and Green Snake travelled in separate directions, moving across the earth to spread the mud and creating mountains and valleys, prairies, and deserts. When Mole and Green Snake met again, the world was covered only in earth and rock. There was no life except Mole and Green Snake.

"Now I will give you the seeds from the sky kingdom and you will spread them across the earth, so that new life will again sprout," said the chief of all creation. Mole and Green Snake took the seeds of creation from the chief and planted them across the earth. It took many years, but the forests eventually returned, the grasslands sprouted up, and the flowers again took over the meadows.

The world again bloomed with life, but it was silent. All across the globe, only Mole and Green Snake walked the lands.

"Oh, great chief," called out Mole. "The world is beautiful and filled with wonderful things to eat but there is no one to talk to. Please send some people down to keep us company and populate these vast lands."

The chief heard Mole's request and called together a council of the people of the sky kingdom. From far and wide the people of the sky travelled to the lodge of their chief.

When everyone had arrived, the chief addressed his people. "The world below is once again whole and peaceful. Those who lived there before were lost in the great fire and flood, but I have repaired the earth and I need you to descend to this world, for great things will come for those who live there."

The chief then began to separate the people of the sky kingdom and send them down to earth. One by one he transformed them into birds, fish, buffalo, deer, bears and all the other animals in the world. He kept all the powerful and great people of the sky kingdom and sent all the rest down to earth. Thus the world was reborn out of fire, water and mud. The earth was again full of life, ready for the chief's greatest creation—the first peoples.